Although not an East E̶ ̶ ̶ ̶s̶ became an honorary 'Iron' courte̶ ̶ ̶ ̶ ̶rable spells with West Ham in the eighties a̶ ̶ ̶ ̶ties. Eleven of his fourteen years of professional football were spent with the Hammers: his legacy there embraced 326 appearances and 65 goals, and he was voted 'Hammer of the Year' in 1990, 1992, 1996 and 1997.

Dicks could certainly play, but it was his presence on the field as a tough-tackling talisman which endeared him to the West Ham faithful. Affectionately nicknamed 'The Terminator', his unstinting aggression, energy and never-say-die attitude embodied the spirit of the club and the pride of its fans.

Dicks also played for Birmingham City, Liverpool and Canvey Island, served on the coaching staff at West Ham, West Bromwich Albion and Watford, and managed Wivenhoe Town, Grays Athletic, West Ham United Ladies and Heybridge Swifts.

Julian Dicks

HAMMER TIME

Me, West Ham, and a Passion for the Shirt

HEADLINE

First published in 2023 by
HEADLINE PUBLISHING GROUP

First published in paperback in 2024 by
HEADLINE PUBLISHING GROUP

1

Cataloguing in Publication Data is available from the British Library.

ISBN: 978 1 4722 9659 7

Designed and typeset by EM&EN
Printed and bound in Great Britain by Clays Ltd, Elcograf S.p.A.

Headline's policy is to use papers that are natural, renewable and recyclable
products and made from wood grown in well-managed forests and other
controlled sources. The logging and manufacturing processes are expected
to conform to the environmental regulations of the country of origin.

HEADLINE PUBLISHING GROUP
An Hachette UK Company
Carmelite House
50 Victoria Embankment
London EC4Y 0DZ

www.headline.co.uk
www.hachette.co.uk

To my late dad

Contents

PART ONE

PART ONE

THE BATH

A wee nip before kick-off

The water's warm, never too hot, and I'm lying in here, stark bollock naked, apart from my football boots.

Outside, the atmosphere is also warming up nicely. Green Street is teeming with people. The Boleyn Tavern can't pull the pints quick enough as the thirsty patrons knock them back, many with whisky chasers. Fans are eating pies quicker than the cafes can bake them. The smell of fried onions and burgers on the mini food stalls alongside the market fills the air.

Not long ago, I was wading my way through that scene, half desperate for a pie and a pint myself, but not today. Or not right now, anyway.

It's 2.40 p.m., and kick-off is only 20 minutes away. And I'm still in the bath.

On the side of the tub are two cans of Coke, and a Mars bar. Or at least they were there a few minutes ago.

Now, the Mars bar and most of the Coke is making its way through my system, hopefully soon to be converted into that endless energy I seem to find when I'm on the pitch. And the other Mars is not long for this world.

As I bite into the chocolate, the sound of the fans coming into Upton Park is getting buzzier and louder.

They're watching the boys warming up, being put through their paces, running, turning, shooting, crossing, all that stuff.

You've probably watched the players do that week in, week out for more years than you can even remember. Ever wondered why they're doing that particular drill? Why they're jumping and jogging, using up all that energy just before a game? Me too.

I've never done a pre-match warm-up, and I never will. They're not for me. At least not on the pitch. On the pitch, I play football. I don't warm up. My warm-up is right here, in the bath with my Coke and Mars.

And as I lie here, I can actually try to chill out, even though the game is just minutes away. You try chilling out in front of thousands of people while doing keepie-uppies or whatever they're doing out there. It's not going to happen.

This is my sanctuary. My place of peace. Until the boys come back in, and the noisy bastards ruin all that, and I have to get out, and get my kit on.

But I don't have to get up for it. I've never understood all that bollocks. The dressing room music, head-butting the walls, screaming in each other's faces. There's no fake way of getting me in the mood to play football. I'm always in the mood to play football. It's all I've ever done, and all I'll ever do.

So never mind the motivational messages from the gaffer, or anyone else, I'm ready to play. I'm ready to die for the *claret and blue. I was ready when I was walking down Green Street before my Coke and Mars bars, and I'll be ready at full-time as well.*

Give me a ball, and I'll play football. That's what I know, and it's who I am.

It's not like the Mars and Coke is even that bad. There's been plenty of brandy knocking around the home changing room for years, and I may even have a nip myself before kick-off.

Go back a few years when Billy Bonds was playing here, and he had his own way of doing things. Billy would be in the gym before a game, block-tackling the wall in there. He'd finish off his routine by head-butting the door a couple of times as well.

I finish the Mars bar, and drain the rest of the Coke, as I think about Billy doing his thing. I have a smile on my face. Those were very different times.

•

At that time, in the late eighties and early nineties, the club physio was Rob Jenkins. I'm not sure what qualifications physios at football clubs required back in the day. His dad had been the physio before him: the Jenkins must have been like some kind of Royal Family for physios where Rob was the next in line.

Not that he would have needed that many qualifications. His physio kit at that time consisted of the magic sponge, a bucket of cold water and a bit of spray. That was it. Oh, and there was also the special brown medicine bottle, the contents of which remained a bit of a mystery.

Rob wasn't shy about passing the bottle around before a game, or even at half-time. On a freezing cold and wet Saturday afternoon, loads of us would have a swig.

That's how it was then. These were the days before the Premier League. Before the branding. Before the razzmatazz, the glitz and the glamour. Before anyone was paid unbelievable amounts of money to play football.

I don't want to sound like an old fart, but they were more simple times. And they were absolutely fucking brilliant.

They were the days when the physio somehow didn't really need any qualifications. It was much more a case of feeling what was required, rather than consulting with any kind of medical authority for the appropriate course of action.

A case in point, was the fantastic night in the 1988/89 season when we played the mighty Liverpool side, boasting John Barnes, Ian Rush and Peter Beardsley to name a few, some of whom would go on to become my team-mates, but that's another story for another chapter.

Upton Park was rocking that evening, and we found something that we could never find in the league that year to beat them 4–1. And this was a season which saw us relegated, and our legendary manager John Lyall sacked.

At 3–1, I got a kick in the head and there was blood everywhere, running into my eye and down my face. Rob came on with his bucket and magic sponge, and did his best to try to patch me up, but there wasn't much he could do. He told me I'd have to come off as it was a deep cut that kept bleeding, so it might need stitches.

'Fuck off!' I told him, as there was absolutely no way I was leaving the pitch and missing any of this game. Alvin Martin double checked that I wasn't going to go off, but he needn't have bothered.

Rob had to think on his feet, so he shoved a load of Vaseline on the cut and gave me a slug from the brown bottle. Job done. And I don't think you'd find any medical professional who would have prescribed that particular course of treatment.

He left the pitch, Tony Gale stepped up to take the freekick that I'd won and curled it into the corner for number four.

Rob was an unbelievable character, to say the least.

He was also someone who had your back – as long as you had his. He had some pretty unusual approaches to rehabbing injured players.

If we were ever crocked, we obviously couldn't play on a Saturday, but we would certainly be expected to come in for treatment on a Sunday. Except if you'd been out on the piss until 4 a.m. on Saturday night, like we had been pretty

7

much 99 per cent of the time, there was absolutely no way in hell that you were going to make it to the training ground on Sunday morning.

I'd often call Rob to explain that I couldn't make it in on a Sunday because I was too worse for wear after a heavy night. 'No problem Julian,' would be his response, followed by: 'I won't tell the gaffer.'

If we kept Rob sweet, on a Monday morning when the manager came in and asked if I'd been in for treatment the day before, he'd tell him we'd been there, working hard on getting fit again.

Not that I've ever been against working hard to get fit, because I have no problem with that. Ask anyone who I've shared a dressing room with, and they'll tell you that I play five-a-side in training like I play a first-team game on a Saturday – and they've probably got the scars to prove it too.

My issue with training is when we don't play with a football – which is exactly why I always warm up in the bath before a game, and not on the pitch. And don't even get me started on running in training, because I utterly detest that particular type of torture. In the early days of my career, I went along with it, because I was too young and too green to know any better.

In fact, when I'd just signed professional forms for Birmingham, we had a unique approach to pre-season training which, thinking about it now, was absolutely insane.

I'd arrived in Birmingham as a spotty 14-year-old, signed as a schoolboy by the great Ron Saunders, who saw something in me despite the fact that I was as skinny as a rake, and not particularly tall. At the time, Ron was the Aston Villa manager, but he soon headed across the city to manage the Blues, and I followed him to St Andrew's, where the likes of Noel Blake, Mick Harford, Tony Coton, Robert Hopkins and Billy Wright were first-team regulars. Ron was way ahead of his time, in so many respects, and he had a ground-breaking attitude to sports nutrition.

I was living in digs and his orders to my landlady were to make sure I had steak twice a week, and a bottle of Guinness every day. I could hardly believe my luck.

I don't know if it was all those steaks and bottles of Guinness, or just my natural development, but it wasn't long before my tiny frame gave way to a slightly bigger physique, and I was rubbing shoulders with those hard nuts in first-team training.

In my first proper pre-season as a pro at Birmingham, we would spend the mornings running in Elmdon Park, which was full of hills. We'd have to run up those hills again and again for around an hour, and by the end of it, we were absolutely battered, with many of us puking at the top of the hill. I hated every second of it.

Then it was back to the training ground where we had an hour for lunch, rest and recovery, before repeating all that running in the afternoon. So you would imagine that

9

precious hour would be spent refuelling, taking plenty of water on board and putting our feet up.

Not in a million years.

In fact, what would happen on a daily basis, was that we'd all pile into the minibus and the kitman would drive us to the nearest pub, where we'd all sink four or five pints, then head back to the training ground.

Those afternoon runs would largely follow the pattern of the morning, as we struggled up the hills, puked at the top, except this time we were throwing up all the beer that was inside us. It's hard to believe that was pre-season in the eighties, but that's how it was. Ron Saunders had no idea where we'd spent our lunchtimes. So many of the players lived locally in Solihull, that he assumed they'd gone home for lunch.

Maybe we could have prepared better for a tough season ahead – ok, we definitely could have done better – but what that did create was an incredible togetherness about us as a team.

It's hard to explain it, but it was so good being part of that team, knowing that we all cared about each other. Yes, we went out and got rat-arsed regularly, but we were putting the spirit into team spirit, and that definitely helped us play better together too.

Even when I was just 14 or 15, those senior players looked after me. I was a fish out of water, having moved from Bristol on my own, only returning home every weekend. So, it was important that I would be treated with love, care and respect from the senior players in the dressing room – perhaps Noel Blake and Mick Harford taking me out to Faces nightclub in Birmingham at the age of 15 was not the best idea, but it showed me I was a part of something, even at that age.

I didn't drink at that point, and it felt great to be out with those lads – the landlord of my digs, Brian, was the manager of the club which is why we always went there – and there was never any trouble. Mind you, someone would've had to be insane to pick a fight with either of those two.

As a Birmingham apprentice, I had to learn fast, especially when it came to cleaning boots. It's an old cliché, but as a youngster that was one of my most important jobs, and if the boots that were my responsibility weren't considered clean enough, I'd know about it.

Wayne Clarke, and the goalkeeper Jim Blyth, would give me a friendly slap across the head if they didn't like the state of the boots I returned to them. But they also had my back. On a baking hot August day, we were in the training ground dressing room, and Ron Saunders was speaking to the team, and got me to wave the door forwards and backwards in order to create a bit of a breeze for everyone.

I must have been going for about 15 minutes, when the boys complained to the gaffer that it wasn't really on making me do that. Which was very considerate of them, but they might have spoken up earlier than 15 minutes in.

Those Birmingham boys kept me grounded, but they also looked after me. If I hadn't grown up so quickly with those players, it's possible I would never have made it as a pro myself.

I certainly don't think I would have settled in at West Ham as quickly. That exact same Birmingham dressing room culture was also present at West Ham, both in terms of the team spirit, and in how much I hated running, especially in pre-season.

That problem got worse for me when my former teammate Billy Bonds eventually became manager because he absolutely bloody loved running.

When Billy moved into the Hammers hotseat, he was determined to make sure that all his players were as fit as he was. Another difficulty for me was that Billy was the fittest player I've ever played with. Even into his 40s, he would run and run and run. I can't tell you how much he loved running, but I can tell you how much I hated it. It was fucking horrendous.

As I always used to say to Billy, 'Let the players play, and let the runners run' because I never understood why footballers like me couldn't just get on with playing football. It pissed me off that I could easily play for 90 minutes, or 120 if necessary, but there were super-fit players who couldn't kick a ball from A to B.

But my protests fell on deaf ears. I was the club captain by that stage, and Billy wanted to see me setting an example to the younger players, which is why he always got right on my case when I was about half a mile off the pace on those pre-season runs. And that was within the first mile.

One morning we'd set off from the training ground in Chadwell Heath, from where we were running a few miles to Hainault Forest then looping back to where we started. From the off, I was at the back with Frank McAvennie. So much so, that by the time we went through the training ground gates, the rest of the players were already about 400 yards up the road. I told you I was off the pace.

Billy Bonds was at the very front, of course, and suddenly we could see him sprinting back towards us. He quickly reached us – which wasn't very hard given how slowly we were moving – and said, 'Fuck me, boys, what are you doing? Come on!' and then he sprinted back to the front, almost effortlessly.

On any run we did, this would happen all the time, as Billy regularly pegged it to the back and yelled at me to get a shift on. 'Let the players play!' would be my comeback, to which the gaffer would respond with something along the lines of 'Fuck off, I can't run this slow!' before jetting back to the front again.

On this particular day, me and Frank had made it to Hainault Forest and were about to begin the long, hot, slog back to the training ground, when a milk float drove past us, and the driver recognised us, calling out, 'Hello lads!'

This was not an opportunity to be missed, so we flagged him down. 'Can you give us a lift back to Chadwell Heath please?' I asked.

'You could run back there faster than this milk float,' he replied.

'Listen, your milk float is faster than me and Frank!' I said as we jumped on board.

As we cruised back towards the training ground, we noticed that Billy had placed some of his coaching staff at strategic points along the way to make sure nobody was cutting corners – or getting lifts on milk floats. So, every time we approached one of the gaffer's spies, Frank and I ducked down into the empty milk crates, like a couple of schoolboys hiding from their teacher. It was unbelievably funny.

We jumped off close to the training ground, before trotting back in, and putting on our best exhausted faces as we went past Billy and headed for a shower.

'Well done boys, fucking great!' he called out, and I couldn't believe we'd got away with it. Showered and dressed, we headed home, feeling like we'd won that particular battle.

Except, shortly after we left the training ground, the coaches returned to raise the alarm to the gaffer that they couldn't find either myself or Frank anywhere, which really confused Billy who had only just seen us leave.

The following morning, Billy called the pair of us into his office to face the music.

'What did you do yesterday?' he asked us. 'How did you get back to the training ground?'

'We fucking ran!' I said.

'Don't lie to me, how did you get back?'

'Ok, we jumped on a milk float,' I confessed, realising that the game was up for us.

'I know you did, do you know why I know?'

'No.'

'Because the milk float you jumped on was our fucking milkman's milk float, and he told me!'

We could see that Billy had a smile on his face, so we couldn't help but laugh ourselves. As rigid and serious as he could be, he also had a good sense of humour and he definitely saw the funny side of our antics.

'Don't let it happen again!' he warned us, as we left his office, relieved not to get too much of a ticking off, although given that it was pre-season, another day of sodding running awaited us.

Billy was totally obsessed by running for fitness. As far as he was concerned, there was no other way to get fit, not even playing football, which was always my preferred method.

He had us doing those bleep tests where you have to run between two points before a bleep sounds. Each time you complete a few runs, the period between the bleeps gets shorter, so it becomes progressively harder. What a load of absolute bollocks. My first reaction to the bleep test was typical of my first reaction to most fitness drills – 'What the fuck is this about? I'm here to play football.'

As well as his bleep test, Billy also used to make us do five-and-a-half laps of the football pitch, which he'd worked out as being a mile. There were people like Martin Allen and Matthew Rush flying round in five or six minutes, much to Billy's delight.

Me? I did it in 17 minutes. It might have been quicker to walk. In fact, I must have been walking. The gaffer came up to me, looking distinctly unimpressed.

'That is not acceptable!'

'Billy, when do you ever run a mile straight off on a football pitch?' I replied.

It just made no sense to me. Here I was, a player who had been substituted literally once in my entire career when I was a youngster at Birmingham, who played every minute of every game for West Ham. And there was a good reason for that – they all knew what they'd get from me on a Saturday.

I could outlast even the fittest players when it came to actually playing football. And, despite all the running, we had plenty of training that did feature football, which massively helped my fitness.

We used to play one-on-one games on a full-size pitch. Seriously. There would be a goalkeeper at either end, and then just two of us going hell for leather against each other. I would be up against Mark Ward, as there weren't any others who could tackle me. When the two of us were on opposing sides in any contest, there were feathers everywhere, as we'd kick the shit out of each other.

And it was exhausting. If I had a shot, the keeper would then throw it out to Wardy who was already on the other side of me, meaning I had to turn and run full sprint to try to catch him. That's how I got my fitness. If Billy had given me a ball to run to Hainault with, I would have been ok.

Five-a-side in training was the same. I didn't hold back, but to be fair, nobody did. We would kick lumps out of each other because that's just the way it was. We were all competitive and trained like we meant it. The mantra was 'you play as you train, and you train as you play'.

At one point, John Lyall called me and Wardy into his office and explained to us that under no circumstances were we ever to be on opposing teams in training. He was concerned that one of us was going to end up with a serious injury as we were flying into tackles on each other without a care in the world.

'Well, it won't be me,' I told him, half-joking. I loved Wardy. He was a funny Scouser, and we were very similar characters in terms of our competitive spirit. Neither of us could tolerate losing, whether it was playing football, cards or tiddlywinks – not that we ever played that. I don't even know what it is.

When David Speedie joined the club on loan in 1993, the same rule was implemented, this time by Billy Bonds. He was a similar kind of character to Wardy, and me and him on opposing sides just didn't work. We just didn't know any way, other than kicking the shit out of each other, so it was quickly decided that we'd have to be on the same team.

Unfortunately, sometimes there were bad training ground injuries, like when I accidentally broke poor Simon Webster's leg.

Simon had come to West Ham from Charlton, and he hadn't been there that long. A summer signing, he never made it through pre-season. During a game in training, I won the ball off him with a block tackle, and I carried on up the pitch and scored a goal.

I celebrated the strike too, because I think there was a fiver per player riding on the game, but when I looked round, Simon was still on the ground. It was a freak accident, as the block tackle had broken his leg really badly and, sadly, his career was extremely limited after that.

There was nothing I could have done about what happened to poor Simon, it was just one of those things that can occasionally happen on a football pitch. I found out that he had previously broken his leg while at Sheffield United, and that the tackle had somehow shattered his leg in the same place again.

Fortunately, although I felt bad about what happened, it didn't dampen my enthusiasm or willingness to play the way I'd always played. And that was the case, whether it was out on the pitch, or a kick-about in the gym. But perhaps I should have been a bit more careful with Tony Gale's little boy, who found out about my competitive spirit the hard way.

Tony was the Hammers centre-back and a good mate, and one Saturday we'd all showered and changed after a match, and some of the lads' families were hanging around in the gym which was not far from the changing rooms at Upton Park.

And when I say families, I mean their kids. The gym was full of kids playing football, but it looked like they were having a lot of fun and I couldn't resist joining in, so I had a quick drink in the Players' Lounge next door, then joined them.

It wasn't long before I was smashing the ball around the gym, in my smart matchday suit, and working up a sweat again, despite just having played 90 minutes of a top-flight game.

Tony's son was eight years old at the time, and clearly a brave lad as he went in goal while I was firing in pot-shots from all over the gym. But he was probably a bit too brave, as he tried to save one of those shots, and started crying because his wrist was hurting.

He ran off to his old man, who wasn't the most sympathetic, but on closer inspection, it turned out that I'd broken the poor boy's wrist.

'Thanks a lot, Dicksy!' was Tony's sarcastic response,

but I did feel for his boy, and for him, as he would have had to explain to his missus that a First Division left-back had broken her son's wrist.

It probably wasn't the only time her boy, and plenty of other kids, were left a bit traumatised by my enthusiasm. We used to do Christmas parties for the kids where we'd have a big bouncy castle with a goal in it, and the children had to chip the ball up into the goal. Except if I was in between the sticks, there was no way the little buggers were going to be getting any free hits. I dived all over the place saving their shots.

Alvin Martin's son, David, also used to go in goal, and I didn't hold back, larruping shots in from 20 yards as hard as I could – it must have set him in good stead as he turned pro many years later. I once tied him up and left him on the bouncy castle unable to move, and everyone was looking for him, not realising what I'd done.

Sometimes, a load of other kids joined him in goal and I'd carry on pounding shots at them so there were balls flying all over the place, including at the kids who had been happily jumping on the bouncy castle. We all seemed to be having great fun, until Tony's wife would tell him to tell me to calm down a little bit.

The funny thing is that I've always got on better with kids than adults – they just want to play football and so do I. At heart, I am probably a great big kid. I was never interested in sitting down for a meal with the adults at those Christmas parties. While the adults were eating and talking, I'd be in the gym kicking the shit out of the kids.

I really couldn't help myself when there was a football involved, just like I couldn't help but not get involved when there was no ball. It got to the point where I just refused to join in with training if we weren't using a ball.

When the coaches would start the training warm-up at 10.30 a.m. and all the lads jogged around the perimeter of the pitch, I didn't join in. Instead, I'd carry a bag of around 20 footballs, and place it down around 30 yards from the goal, then empty out all the balls.

I'd smash every ball into the goal – or close enough to it – go and retrieve every one, stick them back in the bag, then repeat the process all over again. By this point, every-one was stretching, working their groins, hamstrings, calves and lower backs. Not for me.

I thought it was all a load of crap. I would always try to prove to the coaches that there was no point in me doing all that jogging and stretching before a training session, because as soon as we started the five-a-side, I was right in the thick of it, banging in goals, making tackles and leading my team to a handsome victory.

Inevitably, as I walked off the pitch, I'd say, 'I told you that warm-up was crap,' to any of the coaching staff within earshot.

It was the same with practising set pieces. I could never see the point in going over how to attack a corner. If whoever was taking the corners drilled it into the space between the six-yard box and the penalty area, I'd head it in. To me, it was as simple as that, and there was no need to get into any more detail. So when the coaches would set up a corner drill, I'd just walk off and do my own thing.

It wasn't like I was being lazy. The opposite was actually true. I was usually one of the first in at training as I'd get there around an hour before everyone else, so I could smash a ball around in the gym. I loved having that time on my own to hit the ball against targets of my choosing.

There was a clock at one end of the gym, and I once spent some time seeing if I could hit it from the other end of the room. With five balls, I managed to hit it four times, which I was happy about, as it was a fairly small target. I didn't realise that one of the West Ham fanzine editors was watching the whole thing and ended up writing about it – I definitely preferred to do that kind of thing alone.

After training, I would also stay out for an extra half an hour so that I could practise my free-kicks. I couldn't do that on my own, so I'd ask Les Sealey or Ludek Miklosko if they wouldn't mind staying out with me – it wasn't bad practice for them either, to be fair. Les was a fiery kind of character, you never really knew if he'd be up for it or not, but he'd certainly make it as hard as possible for me to score. Once a keeper, always a keeper.

That kind of training routine was scuppered when I moved to Liverpool as they had an old-fashioned rule in place. I couldn't believe that there was a tradition at the club which meant we weren't allowed to play with a ball before or after training. Yes, me, a footballer prevented from using a football, the actual thing that I use for my job. I thought it was absolutely nuts.

At Liverpool's training ground, Melwood, the great Bill Shankly had introduced the rule that footballs were only allowed during the actual training sessions. Because of his legacy, that custom had been adopted by all subsequent Anfield managers.

My own tradition, which admittedly had not gone as far back as the days of Shankly, was to arrive at West Ham training an hour early, at 9.15 a.m. I'd then spend that hour in the gym, clipping balls, chipping balls, smashing balls, whatever I felt like working on really.

So when I turned up at Melwood and discovered that I wouldn't be able to do that, I was far from happy. 'Fuck this,' I thought to myself, 'I'm doing what I want.' So I took a ball and used these boards they had which you could smash balls against, control them, and then hammer them back, like you might do in a game.

The Liverpool manager Graeme Souness had a word and told me it wasn't on. 'Look, you just can't have a ball before training,' he said. 'We don't do that here.'

'Graeme, I'm a fucking footballer!' I pleaded with him.

And to his credit, he let me have my way, but I know it rubbed a few people up the wrong way there. No football before training? I still can't believe that was a rule.

Another thing that Souness couldn't believe was my pre-match routine. Yes, even at Liverpool, I lay in that bath with my Coke and chocolate, which was certainly not something that Shankly would have encouraged either.

There might have been an attempt by the coaches to convince me to get out there with the rest of the lads, but it would have fallen on deaf ears. I think Souness quickly realised I was my own man, which is part of the reason why he signed me to play for him.

It may also have been part of the reason why my spell at Anfield didn't last too long, and I was soon back at West Ham, feeling the true love of the fans who had taken to me from day one, as they recognised something in the way I played the game that spoke to them.

It was a genuine case of love at first sight – well, for the home fans anyway. My West Ham debut was in 1988, on an Easter Bank Holiday Monday, when we played Everton in the First Division in front of 21,000 hardcore Hammers at Upton Park.

My first game for West Ham had been two days earlier in a 2–1 defeat to Sheffield Wednesday at Hillsborough, where the Owls fans had actually voted me as their man of the match, believe it or not. I must have done something right, unless they were taking the piss.

Back in east London, I probably did the warm-up that day, although I'm sure none of the fans were that interested in seeing me run around some cones. I did my talking on the pitch, and that was never truer than on that day.

I had played at the ground before when I was with Birmingham, as a 17-year-old, and the two experiences couldn't have been more different. As an away player at Upton Park, and a young one at that, I was shitting myself, especially whenever I went anywhere near the notorious Chicken Run, the old East Stand, where the fans stood so close to the side of the pitch, that they could touch you – which they often did.

It wasn't the kind of place where you'd have wanted to take a throw-in, as you'd get plenty of abuse as an opposition player. Those fans were working men who paid their hard-earned money to support their team and have a pop at whoever turned up to play against their heroes.

Playing as a Hammer in front of the Chicken Run was a far more pleasant experience. Pats on the back, hugs and plenty of encouragement were normal. Fans there would offer me sweets in the middle of a game, which was lovely but probably a bit too much – I was in the middle of playing.

Why did they love me so much? It started in that game against Everton. Not much happened in the match, which was a goalless draw, but there was one cheer which, if not quite as loud as the noise for a goal, was certainly the most excited the crowd got all afternoon.

It happened when I clashed with Everton's Trevor Steven near the dugouts on the west side of the ground, opposite the Chicken Run as it happens. I gave him a sly elbow, which left him crumpled in a heap on the ground, and the fans went mad. I'm not sure they'd have loved me more if I'd scored a last-minute winner on my home debut. Instead, it was the elbow on Trevor Steven that started our love affair.

And if that sounds brutal, well it was. But this was 1988, when football was a passionate, working man's game. There was very little kissing the badge on the shirt. You had to be aggressive, and you had to look out for yourself. I learned that from playing and training alongside Mark Dennis, Noel Blake and Mick Harford at Birmingham.

At that time, there was only one camera filming every game. And that camera only really went wherever the ball went, which meant you could practically get away with murder off the ball. I can't tell you how many times I got hit by other players, whether it was a punch in the ribs, or a kick on the leg.

That's how the game was. If I went through someone in a tackle, they'd look to get their own back on me, when the ball was up the other end of the pitch. And they'd usually get away with it because everyone else was watching the ball, including the cameraman.

I remember playing in a game at Bradford when I was still a youngster and came up against a huge centre-forward called Bobby Campbell, who was a bit of a cult hero up there, as he scored a lot of goals for them.

We got into a tangle after I cleared the ball, and he tried to kick me, so I gave him a kick. He stared right at me and said, 'I'm gonna get you!'

For the rest of the game, every time they got a goal kick, he would yell at the keeper to 'put it there', pointing to wherever I was on the left, so he could have a chance to nail me. Luckily for me, he never did. But that's exactly how it was. You kick people, you expect to get kicked back.

Or, in my case on my home debut, you elbow people. Trevor Steven never actually got me back, which is just as well or that early reputation I carved out for myself might well have been damaged.

•

I'm thinking about that moment as I lie back on a bed in the medical room. Maybe I'll get another chance to keep that relationship going with the fans this afternoon?

I've moved on from the bath, and the Cokes and Mars bar have now been replaced by a little bit of the contents of Rob's medicine bottle.

There's only a few minutes until kick-off, and it's quite nippy out there today, so I've got to make sure that I'm in the best possible shape to play.

I can hear some of the fans trying to get 'Bubbles' started. The atmosphere is building, which is why it's so important

I keep calm in here, and don't get too pumped up and carried away.

From the changing room, I can now hear the noise of the boots on the floor. My team-mates are in there, fresh from their warm-up, disturbing the peace.

I'm glad I'm in here, staying in my own little world, away from all that noise.

It's time for me to get properly focused now. I need to stay as relaxed as possible, as kick-off is fast approaching.

I hear a few shouts from the dressing room. Someone's trying to get everyone going. Fair enough, that's their way.

I can also hear the faint noise of whatever music is being played around the stadium at the moment – it's only faint because it's struggling to be heard above the noise of the fans out there.

They must be buzzing with anticipation, and so am I, but I'm doing my best to stay calm.

I've known of players drinking pints when the pubs open at noon, before going to play.

Suddenly, something changes. It's the dressing room. The noise quietens down, the players are silent and I can hear another voice. It's the gaffer.

They're all in there together now, listening to a few last-minute instructions before the game.

This is it.

Here we go.

Give it another minute and I'll go and join them.

THE HOTEL ROOM

Fuck it. I'm buying the dog food

I'm lying on a really comfy bed. I've got the TV remote control in my hand, flicking through the channels, trying to find something to watch.

There's not much noise, either in the corridor or from outside. Unusual for a Friday night, and a far cry from a few years ago, when these nights would usually end in some kind of disorder – and I would always be directly involved.

We were bored then. People like Wardy or Frank McAvennie, my old room-mates, were restless and needed to be occupied.

You couldn't leave them or me in a hotel room overnight and expect us to get our heads down for an early night. Not when we had all that nervous energy to burn before a game.

It's different now. First of all, these beds are a lot nicer than the ones we used to sleep on when we first started staying away before a game – and before that, we'd just drive up on the day of the game, so there were no hotels at all.

When I first started playing that's how it was. Unless we were playing Newcastle or Middlesbrough, or another team at the other end of the country. Otherwise, it was an early start on the team bus, and we'd drive up to the Midlands or wherever, everyone playing cards or watching films all the way there.

We'd get off the coach, completely stiff from the journey and would be on the pitch playing pro football a couple of hours later. Nobody ever thought it wasn't a great idea, it was just how it was done, mainly because there wasn't a lot of money in the game, and clubs had to save where they could.

When we started staying overnight for most away games, everything became a lot more fun, certainly in terms of the bond and banter between the team. There was a lot more opportunity to piss about, which I've always believed was great for team spirit.

I miss those times, and those characters. You don't realise at the time what an absolute buzz it is to spend every weekend with your mates, and that it's also your job.

There are so many memories of those away trips, and almost all of them involve doing stupid things to relieve the boredom.

Some of these memories fly through my mind as I lie here, aimlessly flicking through more TV channels. There's no end to them these days.

I turn to my bedside table and pick up the bottle of Jack Daniel's. Never mind American Express, I don't leave home without this.

I pour a little bit into the glass that's next to my bed, then I pull out a can of Coke from my bag, and stick a bit of that in the glass too.

I take a sip from the glass, and taste that magic combo that I've been having at this time every week for years. Some things never change.

I reach out onto the bedside table, take a cigarette out of the packet that's lying next to the bottle, and light it up. Glorious.

This has always been a part of my pre-match routine, and always will be. The hotel rooms change, as do the team-mates, but not the rituals.

Us footballers are a strange breed. We have our habits and we like to stick to them. If it works, it works.

That's why we might pull on one sock or one boot before the other, every time, no matter what. Even if we lost last week and the superstition doesn't make sense, there's still some comfort in the repetition.

I take another drag of the cigarette, while still looking for something to watch on the telly. No change there either. More channels, nothing to watch.

I lift the glass that's still in my hand to my mouth and have another sip. It tastes so good, that I gulp the lot down in one go.

When my room-mate gets back, I might put some music on as we share the same tastes, especially if he's gone to the effort of bringing a ghetto-blaster with him.

A bit of Guns N' Roses, with another JD and Coke maybe? Don't mind if I do.

I can't do an away game without the JD. It's just my way

of dealing with the night before a match. It's not like I'm going to get absolutely plastered. It's just a few drinks in my room. Very low key.

Tomorrow is different, of course. There'll be no alcohol until we're back on the coach after the game.

The game, the game. I'm thinking about it now, and I'm excited to get out on the pitch again, but not exactly nervous. I'm up for it.

When I think about some of the madness that went on a few years back, a few JD and Cokes, and a smoke is pretty tame by comparison.

I lie my head even further back into my pillow than it was before, and those memories are all there again.

•

It's the stupidity of all those antics that I find most amusing looking back now. We must have been particularly bored to come up with some of the stuff, but also extremely creative. How many funny stories do you know that feature the use of chocolate buttons and an iron as props?

Mark Ward was one of my regular room-mates. As I explained, we were quite similarly competitive characters, both on and off the pitch. I liked how feisty he was, and I think the feeling was mutual.

I think we were playing away to Hull, but it doesn't really matter. It really wasn't about the football. We'd had dinner, and we were back in our rooms for the night.

Back then, the hotel room was pretty basic. We had two single beds with a cabinet in between them, there were some other cupboards and a TV. We also had an en suite shower room and toilet.

The deal was whoever got in the room first, would claim the prized TV remote control, and keep hold of it for as long as possible. On this particular occasion, Wardy had beaten me to the room.

I was lying on my bed, he was on his, with the remote control in his hand, flicking through the channels. And when I say flicking through the channels, he was actually giving me a headache as he wouldn't settle on any one of them. He just kept going.

And what you really have to remember about this is the fact that at that time, there were only four channels to choose from anyway.

'Wardy, put something on the TV!' I yelled.

'Fuck off, you prick,' came his reply, but it was said in jest rather than in any malicious way. That was simply how we talked to each other.

He continued flicking from BBC1 to BBC2, then to ITV, and Channel 4, before going back to BBC1, and repeating the process again and again.

'You scouse twat! I'm gonna iron my clothes,' I said, as I got off the bed, and went to look for the iron.

We always wore suits on a matchday, and I was very particular about how I looked, so I always made sure that my shirt was ironed, trousers pressed. Those things were important to me. But not as important as putting Wardy in his place.

As I started to iron, he got off his bed to go for a shower, which got me thinking. It didn't take long to conjure up a simple plan. It wasn't really a plan, if I'm being honest, more of a spontaneous moment when I was greeted by the site of a naked Wardy emerging from the bathroom.

Quick as a flash, as he walked past me, I lifted the iron up and planted it squarely on his arse. The thing must have been as hot as the sun, and as I pulled it off his bum, there were bits of his skin all over the iron.

He went absolutely fucking mental, running around the room screaming and shouting, completely understandably. After a few seconds of that, he pegged it straight back into the bathroom to cool his butt cheek down under a cold shower.

'That's what you get for fucking about with me,' I said to him, as he returned to his bed, still moaning, as I went off for my shower. As the hot water poured down on my head, I began to be concerned about exactly how he'd have his revenge.

As I stood there, I was visualising returning to the room, and seeing my clothes all cut up into dozens of pieces on my bed. Then, I considered the possibility of looking out of the window, to see my bedding in the front garden of the hotel. At the very least, surely, my trainers would be up on the roof? There was no way he was going to take this lying down.

But as I emerged from the shower, that was exactly what he was doing, as he was still on his bed, and nothing had happened. My clothes were where I'd left them, the bed and bedding were all intact and there were my shoes, exactly where I'd put them under the bed.

Pleasantly surprised, I thought to myself 'the little prick has learned his lesson' and I got into bed to go to sleep because it was getting late by then.

Before I knew it, it was about 8 a.m. and time for us all to get our arses, or a very sore, red arse in the case of Wardy, out of bed for breakfast.

Before I'd even opened my eyes, like most blokes, I had a quick scratch of my bollocks and straightaway something didn't feel right. I felt a disgusting, soft substance all over my hand, and instantly pulled it up to my face for closer inspection.

To my horror, I was greeted by an awful brown mess all over my hand. Sheer blind panic took over for a few seconds, as I didn't know what to make of it.

'Fuck it,' I thought to myself. 'I've shit the bed!'

Just as I was being absolutely gripped by the fear of what I might have done in my sleep, I heard Wardy quietly chuckling from his bed. Something was not right here.

With enormous trepidation, I bravely pulled my hand close to my nose so that I could smell the brown stuff. It only took half a second for a wave of relief to wash straight through me, when I realised that the substance was definitely not shit, but actually chocolate.

While I'd been in the shower the previous night, the sly bastard had put little chocolate buttons all over my bed, and over the course of the night they'd melted all over my bottom half, covering me in what looked suspiciously like shit. I had to hand it to him. It was a class move.

But not as classy as my next one, which was to leap out of my bed and squat on his face with my arse, leaving him with chocolate all over his mug. At least I think it was chocolate.

Fortunately, we could both wash the chocolate off, but Wardy's arse remained on fire and he had to play against Hull with a bit of cream from the physio Rob Jenkins, and a tremendous amount of discomfort I'd imagine.

It might sound like a ridiculous excuse, but incidents like that were born out of pure boredom. We didn't have much to entertain us, so we made our own fun.

There was always a danger of boredom on those overnight trips, but I did my best to make sure that wasn't the case. Most of my West Ham team-mates used to call me Norm, or Dicksy. Nobody at the club ever really called me The Terminator, as much as I would have enjoyed that, although it was a name that the fans used for me.

Norm came from a pre-season trip to Norway one summer. While we were there, loads of the lads decided to venture out and do some sightseeing, and they asked me if

I wanted to join them. 'Sightseeing? Fuck off!' was my succinct response to that. Why the hell would I have wanted to do that? That did not sound like much fun at all.

Instead, I made my way to the hotel bar, and perched on a stool right at the end of it. When they all came back, they marched through the bar, and Tony Gale could see me sitting there, probably not in my most flattering position. He called out 'Norm!' and I looked up, and everyone laughed, with the joke being that I looked like the fat fucker sat at the bar on the TV show *Cheers* which was popular at the time. And, in those days, I wasn't shaven-headed, and my hair was quite wavey believe it or not, completing the Norm look.

From that point on, I was Norm. To be fair, I used to carry a bit of weight, certainly a hell of a lot more than I did when I was 14 and newly arrived in Birmingham, and Ron Saunders put me on my steak and Guinness 'diet'.

I never looked back from those early skinny rake days, but I must've overdone it ever so slightly. I remember my first day at West Ham, Tony greeted me by telling me 'You're a bit fat!' which was nice. It was all part of the banter. Although you don't necessarily expect it from your manager too.

When 5 ft 6 Lou Macari took over from John Lyall at Upton Park, I met him for the first time when we passed each other at the training ground. He looked me up and down and said, 'You're quite fat,' so I replied, 'And you're a fucking midget!'

He might have had a point though, as I was probably

guilty of carrying a little bit of timber throughout my career. After my first very long injury lay-off when I was out for well over a year, I came back to the first team after only playing one warm-up game.

My normal playing weight was probably around 12 stone and 12 pounds, but I was well over 14 stone that day – and admittedly I gave away a goal with a mistake, but made up for it by scoring a penalty.

So maybe I did carry some extra weight, but it didn't make a whole lot of difference back then. Look at Jan Molby at Liverpool. Not exactly lean, was he? Micky Quinn at Newcastle was definitely on the large side, and he banged in an unbelievable amount of goals.

It really didn't matter, and that's because things were very different at that time, and some of the stuff we got up to just wouldn't happen nowadays because the game has changed so much. You can't imagine two players escaping out of their team hotel and then trying to make it across a six-lane dual carriageway, just for kicks, can you?

But that's exactly what me and John Moncur did late one night before an away game. I was sharing a room with my old mate Martin Allen that night. He was brilliant to share with, the kind of bloke you could have a laugh with, and he wasn't shy when it came to taking the piss, meaning we got on well.

I have no idea where he was on that particular night, but he wasn't in the room, and I was having a drink with Moncs.

Now, John was a very good mate of Gazza's and they were cut from the same cloth, as he was also bonkers. He did so many ridiculous things, I can't even remember half of them. Trust me, the bloke was a genuine lunatic.

On that particular evening, I was feeling very restless, as often happened on those away trips. There's a whole load of nervous energy flying around before a game, and we were always looking for ways to burn it off by amusing ourselves.

'I'm fucking bored, John,' I said. 'Let's go over the road to the garage.'

He looked out of the window that I was staring out of. Outside there were three busy lanes of a dual carriageway, followed by the massive 6 ft high barrier of the central reservation which was separating the traffic from another three lanes of dual carriageway. Beyond that was the garage, our holy grail, where we might find a porno mag or book to entertain us.

We looked further down the road, and in the distance it looked like there was a junction where we could cross safely but that was around half-a-mile away, meaning we would be looking at a round trip of a mile.

John looked at me, nodded, and within a minute we were dodging speeding cars and heading to the middle of the road. We scampered up the barrier, over the other side of it, then dodged more cars to finally make it to the garage. Job done.

Except when we got in there, we were greeted by the sight of not very much at all. The only things to buy in there were some chocolate and a massive 5 kg bag of dog biscuits, the sort that expand when you chuck water over them.

Our disappointment was obvious, but I tried to make the best of the situation.

'Fuck it,' I said. 'I'm buying the dog food.'

'What the fuck are you gonna do with that?' asked John.

'I don't know.'

Back we went over the barrier, this time armed with my 5 kg bag of dog food, over the dual carriageways, and into the hotel.

We got back to my room, and Martin still wasn't there. I had no clue where he was or what he was doing, but I certainly sensed my opportunity. I stripped back the duvet and blanket on his bed, and chucked the entire contents of the dog food bag onto his sheets. I then poured about a gallon of water over the dog food, ensuring it expanded into the mushiest mess imaginable.

I made the bed up again, because at heart I was a neat and tidy kind of man, and then John and I waited for Martin to return.

As I heard the door of the room opening, I jumped into my bed, and John lay down the side of the bed. We kept quiet, and eventually Martin got into bed, but he didn't stay in there very long. He went absolutely fucking nuts. 'What the fuck have you done?' he yelled, as John and I started wetting ourselves laughing.

We put the lights on, and Martin was covered in wet

dog food, looking far from happy. He calmed down soon enough, got cleaned up, but there was one problem I hadn't really thought about – if I'm honest, I hadn't really thought about any of it – and that was the fact that he had nowhere to sleep.

I didn't really want to face the hotel staff and try to explain what had happened at that point. Instead, I had the pleasure of sharing a bed with Martin Allen for the night, which was certainly not the most comfortable night's sleep for either of us. I presume John Moncur removed himself from down the side of my bed, but you never know with him.

Poor old Martin was also in the firing line when we played Oldham away. He came out of his hotel room on the Saturday, ready to get on the team bus. He looked immaculate in his West Ham tracksuit, with his hair brushed back, and his bag slung over his shoulder. He really looked the part.

But not for long. I noticed a food tray on the floor outside his room because he'd obviously been tucking into his own pre-match meal. There was a small plate with a few wedges of half melted butter on it, so I covered my hand in the butter and then rubbed my hand right through his beautifully brushed hair.

With the bag over his shoulder occupying his hands, he couldn't have really done much about it and, with the team bus minutes away from leaving for Boundary Park, there was very little he could do in terms of cleaning up his hair.

I couldn't stop laughing when Martin got on the bus, with his hair still encased in greasy butter. He shook his head at me but gave me a wry smile, to let me know that he was ok about it. Sort of. He was a decent bloke.

If you think I was harsh, then Moncs didn't seem to have any kind of filter, and there was nothing he wouldn't do for a laugh. He was crackers. He once turned up to training a bit late and found that all his gear had been nicked, which was something that kept happening to him back then.

For reasons only he will know, he decided that the best course of action was to remove all his clothes, cover himself in paint, then put a little slip on, before joining all of us on the training pitch.

Harry Redknapp was the gaffer at the time and his understandable reaction to John was, 'What the fuck are you doing?'

'I've got no training gear, gaffer,' explained Moncs. 'Nobody's given me anything to wear!'

There was a lot of laughter from the lads, but nothing like that coming from Harry, who was aware that there were a few fans watching training that day, and obviously wanted to show them a professional set-up.

There was no chance of that with Moncs around. He was also capable of much, much worse, like an unforgettable incident at QPR.

We were playing at Loftus Road, where they had plenty of single baths, so I could perform my usual pre-match ritual of a good soak, with my Cokes and Mars bar. I ran myself a lovely bath with bubbles in it, and before I put my boots on, I stepped my feet into it.

I glanced down into the tub, and I was stunned to see a shit floating in it. I turned my head towards the doorway, and a load of the lads were standing there laughing their heads off. Even the coaching staff were laughing. John Moncur had done a shit in my bath.

Really, there are no words to describe a character like that. Apart from absolute fucking lunatic. He also repeated that particular trick in Martin Allen's bath. Like I said, Moncs was very similar to Paul Gascoigne, who I shared a room with when I was called up to play for England Under-21s.

I first met Gazza when I was playing in the FA Youth Cup for Birmingham, and we got drawn against Newcastle. It was a two-legged tie, and there was a lot of talk about Gazza in the papers before the first game at St Andrew's, because he'd already been around the first team.

They beat us 2–1 that night, and I remember thinking to myself after the game that he was a decent player, but he wasn't *that* good. That was until the second leg, when we went up to St James' Park and they hammered us 7–1, with Gazza running the game from start to finish. He was un-believable, absolutely incredible. After that game, I revised my opinion to 'Fuck me, what a player he is.' He was on another level.

You couldn't get at him on the pitch, as he always had a smile on his face, even if you kicked him. He'd just get up and smile or laugh at you. In fact, he'd often say 'Come and get me, come on then!' which really made me want to kick him even more. But it made no difference. He was a player like no other, from a completely different planet.

He spent a lot of his time off the pitch inhabiting a different planet too, as I found out when we both played for England in the 1988 Toulon tournament in France.

When we arrived at the team hotel, the manager Dave Sexton gathered us to sort out the rooms. He casually asked, 'Who wants to share with Gazza?' and was not met by the greatest response, so I put my hand up and said, 'Go on then.'

Maybe I shouldn't have been so ready and willing. The thing about Gazza is that he was the most brilliant bloke, incredible fun to be with, always laughing. There is nothing he wouldn't do for you; he would give you his last fiver if you needed it. And he obviously loved a drink so we got on very well.

But the only problem with him as a room-mate was that he just did not sleep. Which really didn't bode well in terms of me getting any rest. And when he didn't sleep, he also had to keep himself entertained.

There was one day when I looked up to see him leaning out of the window in our room. We were only a storey or two up, but he was hanging out of the window holding a tube of toothpaste, squirting it at whoever was passing by below.

'What are you doing?' I asked him.

'Oh, just having a bit of fun,' was his reply.

The mad part is he would get away with that kind of thing. If anyone looked up to see why toothpaste seemed to be raining down on them from the skies above, they would see Paul hanging out of the window and think, 'Oh right, it's just Gazza doing his thing.'

Even if I did manage to fall asleep, with Gazza as a room-mate there were no guarantees I would be allowed to remain dozing. One night when I was enjoying my kip, I didn't know it but Gazza was busy preparing a little show for me.

The crazy Geordie had bought loads of firecrackers, and had carefully lined them up around the rim of the toilet, before lighting them all. You cannot imagine how loud the noise was that woke me up. I absolutely shit myself, sprang out of bed, ran straight out of the room and into the hotel corridor, without a stitch of clothing on, with my hands covering my privates.

I was convinced a bomb had gone off, until I saw Gazza emerge from the room laughing his head off. Pretty soon, the hallway was full of people. Not only were there other players and coaches, who had come out to see what all the fuss was about, but there were England bigwigs and their wives, who had also come out of their rooms. And all of them had been greeted by the same view, which was me standing in the middle of the corridor, totally naked, with my hands protecting my modesty. What a sight that must have been.

Once again, Gazza got away with it, as I ended up taking most of the blame for it. I actually think there was a good chance that episode contributed to the dim view that was taken of me by the England management in years to come, helping to tarnish my reputation which meant I never received a full England cap, or call-up.

Not that Gazza would have been remotely bothered about that. The player he was, nobody would ever have a go at Paul so he had licence to get up to a lot more mischief than anyone else did. He was such good fun though, and just brightened up any dressing room. He also brightened up the tournament itself. We had a great squad including Alan Shearer, Vinny Samways and Michael Thomas. Unfortunately, I got sent off in the quarter-final after two industrial challenges which the referee didn't take too kindly to. The problem was that the opponents were pretty good at rolling around on the floor and screaming after I'd kicked them, which definitely didn't help my cause. It was nothing like playing in England, and the refs fell for it every time.

After being suspended for the semi-final which we won, I was back in for the final which was against France, but we lost 4–2 with two of their goals clearly offside. Everyone was gutted not to have won, and I was absolutely fuming when we got back into the dressing room.

I smashed a football that was near the dressing room door, and it accidentally hit a bucket of water which went everywhere. Oops. Dave Sexton was not impressed: 'Do that again and I'll knock you out,' he said.

'Come on then, knock me out!' I foolishly replied before it all got broken up by a few players and coaches who were standing around us. He didn't speak to me again, or even say goodbye when we returned to England, so that also didn't do my international hopes much good.

I found out later that Dave actually used to be a very decent amateur boxer, so it's probably a good job I didn't square up to him because he probably would have been as good as his word and knocked me out.

I think I was quite lucky to get the nod for that tournament, given how I'd snubbed England when the national team had first come calling. I was a young player at Birmingham then, and John Bond was in charge at St Andrew's, when he got the request for me to join up with the England Under-19 squad.

He called me into his office to tell me the good news and, for a second, I was quite proud of myself, seeing this as the beginning of a career full of international call-ups. How wrong I was.

'You're not going,' said John, in a very matter of fact way, as only he could.

'Why not?' I asked him.

'Because they play shit football!'

And that was that. There was no arguing with John Bond. If he didn't want me to join up with England then I wasn't going and that was the end of it.

So after that no-show, I really didn't do myself any favours in Toulon a couple of years later, when I got a red card and then almost ended up fighting the manager.

Amazingly, despite all that, Lawrie McMenemy still selected me for an England B international in Russia in 1992. We were there with the A squad too, who were also playing a friendly in Moscow. I was quite happy playing with the B's, as we had David Seaman, Peter Beardsley, Neil Webb, David Rocastle and Matt Le Tissier among our number, so it was a decent level.

But when I got out there, England manager Graham Taylor came up to me out of the blue and told me that I was going to play in the first team. I couldn't believe it, and I called my mum and dad to tell them the good news.

The games were being played on consecutive nights, with the B game first, so I was quite surprised when I played in that one, which was a 1–1 draw. I thought that two games in two days might be a bit of a stretch for me, but when the team was announced for the following night's international, my name was nowhere to be seen.

Instead, Graham had selected Andy Sinton to play at left-back. You know, Andy Sinton, the right-winger. Yeah, exactly. I just thought, 'For fuck's sake,' but I had to accept it, as Graham obviously had his own ideas. But I still have no clue as to why he told me I was going to play in the first team.

Off the pitch in Russia, it wasn't an especially lively trip, although I did get into a run-in with Lawrie, who was a bit of a disciplinarian. It was the night before the B game, and loads of us were sitting around a table in the hotel at 10 p.m. Nobody was drinking, not even Norm.

Lawrie came over and said, 'Right, everyone to bed.' I thought, 'What?' and said as much to him.

'You've got to go to bed,' he said.

'But it's 10 o'clock,' I protested.

'Yeah, you've got to go to bed.'

'I'm not being funny,' I said, 'but I'm married and I've got two kids, why am I gonna go to bed at 10 p.m.? I'm not drinking or anything.'

'No, you've got to go to bed,' was his firm response.

There was a bit of a stand-off between me and Lawrie as, although most of the lads did as they were told, and sloped off to bed, I was left sitting at the table on my own as a point of principle. It wasn't much fun though.

I just felt we were being treated like kids for no reason. The best managers are the ones that trust their own players and let them set off firecrackers in the toilet. Well, kind of.

When I played club football, I'd always go to bed at 1 a.m. or 2 a.m., because of all the adrenaline the night before a game. Apparently, that wasn't the case with England.

Graham Taylor's false promise was as close as I came to a

senior call-up, although a few years later I bumped into John Gorman, Glenn Hoddle's assistant when he was in charge of England, who had some unusual advice for me if I wanted to get into the team.

We were both in Tenerife one summer, and I was going into Lineker's Bar, as he was leaving, so we met on the stairs. He said to me if I wanted to play for England, I had to let my hair grow on my closely shaven head. 'Fuck off!' I replied, and walked straight past him into the bar.

I was thinking to myself, 'You've got drug abusers, alcoholics and wife-beaters all playing for the national team, and you're telling me to grow my hair!' Making a stupid comment like that was a sign to me that they didn't really want me anyway. John actually denies saying it to me, but my recollection differs.

Without any more England call-ups, my international kicks came in the shape of club tours, including one where West Ham went to Australia at the end of the season.

We'd comfortably stayed up in that campaign, finishing well above the relegation zone so it was like a reward for us, although many of us weren't particularly thrilled about spending 24 hours on a plane.

Personally, I had the added bother of having my ankle in a cast as I'd broken it a few weeks before. I wasn't going to be playing, but the club wanted me to go with them anyway as we were going to do a lot of promotional work out there as well.

Fortunately, we devised a way to make that long journey far better. The club had given us a choice of getting on a coach to the airport or making our own way there – we went for our own option, a limousine.

Loads of us piled into it including Trevor Morley, Kenny Brown, Ian Bishop and Don Hutchison, and in the couple of hours it took to get to the airport we consumed enough beer and champagne to make sure we were pissed before we'd even checked in.

When we arrived at Heathrow, someone opened the door of the limo and a bottle of champagne fell out of the car. The carnage continued on the plane as we stayed well-oiled, taking full advantage of the fact that Frank Lampard Sr and the club's managing director Peter Storey were in charge of the trip, as Harry Redknapp was due to meet us further down the line in Australia.

We had a stop-off in Singapore on the way, where we were allowed to go out for the night, meaning the party could continue. However, when I tried to join the lads in a nightclub, the bouncer wouldn't let me in because of my cast, which ran from my toes all the way up to just below my knee.

I told the boys I would go and see the club doctor to find out if I could cut the cast off, so I headed back to the hotel to find him. All he had was a kitchen knife to work with, but he managed to get the job done, carefully cutting the cast off without sticking the kitchen knife into my leg – all because I really wanted to go clubbing with the rest of the boys. I made it back to the club and was welcomed in by the bouncer.

There were a few funny looks from Frank the next day, who must have wondered what had happened to my cast, but I kept quiet as I didn't want to get the club doctor in trouble.

Once we arrived in Australia, the piss-up continued, although we did play three or four games too. In one of them we were up against Stan Lazaridis who would go on to become a Hammer because of that tour.

Since we were so far away, I thought it was worth seeing all the sights in Australia, including the Sydney Opera House. But whenever I think of that, I also can't help thinking about John Moncur, who got someone to take a photo of him mooning outside the world-famous building.

By the end of the tour Harry had joined us, and he was livid with the performance in the last friendly match which we'd lost, and threatened to ban us from ending the trip on the Gold Coast which we were all looking forward to. Luckily, it was all paid for already, so there was nothing he could do, and the party went on for those last few days too.

Australia was very unusual for us as a club, and was a far cry from Bournemouth which is where we spent quite a few pre-seasons, because of Harry's connection with that part of the country. While all our rival clubs were enjoying the sunshine in Spain and Portugal, we were on the south coast – but we definitely made the most of it.

There was one particular year that stands out, when we were staying in Ferndown Golf Club which also had its own hotel. One night, we were eating at an Italian restaurant, and we were all fairly drunk, when someone threw some food across the table. In the blink of an eye, there was an enormous food fight, and the restaurant walls were suddenly covered in pasta, roast potatoes and pizza. We were banned from that place for life, and Harry was far from happy.

Back at the hotel, I was sharing a room with Jimmy Quinn, and the pair of us trashed Ian Bishop and Trevor Morley's room. We didn't actually break anything, but by the time we'd finished in there, their beds were standing up against the wall, and it was not a pretty sight.

The next day, Jimmy and I went into our room to find the wardrobe wedged into our bathroom. Trev and Bish had taken their revenge. The problem was that the cupboard was so big, and so stuck, that we couldn't get it out of the bathroom. They'd squeezed it in there, good and proper.

So for the privilege of being able to get into our own bathroom, we had to break the cupboard into pieces. Unfortunately, me and Jimmy then received a bill for £800 for the wardrobe, but I refused to pay as I hadn't done it. In the end, everyone chipped in for it.

Harry went absolutely nuts with all of us after that particular trip, which proved to be our last to the south coast, as our behaviour didn't reflect very well on him. The majority of us were fined for our antics.

Jimmy and myself had a fair bit of history as mates and room-mates, and the wardrobe incident was not the only scrape we got into. Before one away game against Swindon, Jimmy had brought his golf clubs along to the team hotel, as he was going to stick around and play with some local mates the day after the game.

For reasons best known to him, he asked me and Frank McAvennie, who I was sharing with at the time, if he could put his golf bag in our room – it might have been because he was sharing with Martin Allen and he could have been worried about what Martin might do with his gear. Weird that he didn't feel that way about me and Frank.

As Frank likes to say, me and him have a very low threshold for boredom, and there wasn't much going on that evening, so we decided to open the bag, get a few clubs and balls out, and have some fun.

Despite not being able to play golf at the time, we still thought we'd set up a game where we were trying to chip the balls into the metal wastepaper bin, via the wall next to the door.

This went on for a while, but we were hopeless at it, shanking the balls left and right, and making a hell of a racket at the same time. It was time for a new game. This time, I opened the window, and the challenge was to see if we could bounce the balls straight out of it. We were a lot better at that and, by the end, we'd managed to lose every single ball from Jimmy's bag.

In the middle of all this, there was a knock at the door, which we ignored at first. But the knocking kept going so we answered the door, and found the gaffer Billy Bonds standing there. He must have heard the commotion, or had possibly seen golf balls flying out of the window.

'What the fuck are you doing?' he said, as he walked into the room, and looked at the scene of golf equipment all over the floor.

His face actually looked quite relieved, so goodness knows what he was imagining, and he swiftly turned around, held his hands up in the air and said, 'I don't want to know,' and left us to it. As he walked out of the room, Frank and I turned around to each other, and started pissing ourselves laughing.

•

I'm laughing to myself, while I think about these stories, lying here on my comfy bed. No doubt, those were great times, some of the happiest of my life.

I take another swig of my second glass of JD and Coke, and I've still got a smile on my face, thinking about Gazza, Martin, Frank, Wardy, Jimmy and everyone else.

As amazing as it is being a footballer, it's also the times off the pitch that I look back on so often.

I pick up the remote and flick through the channels again, looking for something half decent to watch. But it's still all crap.

I get up to go to the loo. While I'm in the bathroom, I can hear the hotel room door open.

'Hello mate!' I call out.

'Hello,' says a voice.

I flush the loo, wash my hands, and get back in the room. There's a bottle of wine on the table in the middle of the room now. I clock it, look up at my room-mate and smile. 'Get in,' I say.

I get back on my bed, and my mind drifts back to those funny times. I know that some of the behaviour doesn't sound great, but I honestly think those were the moments that made all the difference on the pitch.

Whether we would win or lose would often come down to team spirit, and how much effort we were willing to put in for each other.

And even though ironing someone's arse or putting dog food in a bed are both ridiculous things to do, they do also have the effect of strengthening those bonds between all of us.

We weren't the best team, and we often flirted with relegation, but sometimes the difference between staying up and going down might have been due to the togetherness we developed when we were on these trips.

At least that's my excuse, anyway.

THE PENALTIES

Small goal. Big heart

Fuck me! This is absolute shit. Proper pony. We're getting a proper seeing to here in our own back yard.

I am so pissed off. Yes, Man United are a far better team than West Ham, and will always expect to beat us. But we're West Ham and this is Upton Park. We should at least be giving them a game. Instead, we're 2–0 down with 15 minutes left.

I look to my right and the boy wonder David Beckham is lying on the floor next to the goal, celebrating, and Phil Neville has dived right on top of him. Ryan Giggs comes in for a hug too, while Eric Cantona pats him on the back.

Those names. Those players. This team.

But bollocks to all that. I'm fuming because we should be doing a whole lot better than this.

Ole Gunnar Solksjaer scored the first, before Beckham's ridiculous chip from outside the penalty area made it two, and we're now staring down the barrel of a defeat.

Against most teams, I'd back us to still have a sniff even at 2–0 late in the game. Especially in front of our own fans. But this United team are unbelievably good.

The fact that we were 0–0 for nearly an hour is actually a credit to us. But that doesn't make me feel any better right now. I wipe the side of my mouth with my shirt as we prepare to kick-off again.

We have to keep going. I look up to the stands where there are thousands of folks who've spent their hard-earned cash on watching us. I owe it to them, to myself and my team-mates.

They're still roaring us on, we're still playing. Come on, Dicksy, there's still time!

Florin Raducioiu takes the centre. Harry brought him on to try to make an impact when we were a goal behind, but suddenly we're two down.

He's a top lad, but this is his first taste of English football, and he's not used to the physical side of it at all – even after a few training sessions with me.

We push up, so I move into the United half. I'm breathing hard, but I can barely even feel it as I'm so focused on the game.

The ball's in the middle, and comes across to Iain Dowie, who rolls it across to me. In situations like this, there's no time to think, so I don't.

Instead, I see Raducioiu ahead of me near the edge of the United box, and play the ball straight to his feet. Come on Florin, son, hold this up for us, and we might be able to create a chance here.

I can see he's got Ronny Johnsen breathing down his neck,

so I press further forward to receive the ball back from him if he can get there first.

He doesn't control the ball, instead it runs past him, and he rolls around Johnsen – from nowhere, Florin is clean through on goal.

It's happening so quickly. Peter Schmeichel comes off his line to narrow the angle and make himself huge like he always does, but the ball's already flying past him into the far corner of the net.

It's an unbelievable strike. Upton Park erupts with noise. Raducioiu salutes the fans, while I clench my fist and head back to our half. This is not the time for celebrations, we need to use every second that's left.

We're back in the game, and the stadium feels like it's shaking because there's so much noise from the 25,000 fans packed inside here.

I'm buzzing now, and if my team-mates are feeling anything like I am, I know we can do this.

United kick off again and I'm straight into action, bombing forward to cut out any threat down our left.

Very quickly, we win the ball back and Ilie Dumitrescu has it in the middle of the park. I start to move forward, as he plays an excellent through-ball to Michael Hughes, who's suddenly on his own in the penalty area, with only the keeper to beat.

Go on, Michael! Go on! I can hardly breathe, but again that doesn't even matter. The noise is deafening as Michael takes the ball around Schmeichel, but the keeper takes him out and the referee Peter Jones points to the spot.

Oh my god. It's a penalty. The roar around Upton Park is huge. You'd have thought we'd just equalised. Everyone's going mental – everyone that is, except me.

My heart is now absolutely racing because this is all going to be down to me. All the pressure is now on me. I can score this spot kick and draw us level with Man United, Cantona, Double winners, the whole thing.

The truth is I love this. I absolutely love this. The pressure, the atmosphere, the intensity. Moments like this are why I play football. And this is a big moment, and I know it.

I try to stay calm as I walk towards the penalty area, where Schmeichel has his hands on his hips in disbelief.

Externally, I am a picture of calm, but my mind is racing. I know I have to do what I've done so many times before, so I try to focus on smashing that ball into the net as hard as I possibly can.

Ilie Dumitrescu and Michael Hughes hug, actually hug! We've not scored yet! Then Hughes high fives Dowie – Michael did well, but the job is not done yet. I've still got work to do here.

I'm on the edge of the box, and feel a little tap on my shoulder. I turn around and Cantona is standing there. What the fuck does he want?

'Dicks,' he says in his strong French accent, 'small goal!'

I point to my chest and reply, 'Eric, fucking big heart!'

I've no idea where that has come from. It's probably pure adrenaline. Anyway, I'd better not miss now or that cheeky sod will have got one over on me.

I grab the ball and place it on the penalty spot. Schmeichel is standing on his goal-line, and wiping his sweaty face with one of his gloves, then the other.

I turn my back to him, and walk diagonally about five yards, before turning around. I'm ready. This is it. Schmeichel wipes his face again, this time on his shirt sleeve. He must be feeling it.

I'm ready to do it. Come on ref, just blow that whistle. I'm ready to spring off my front foot and start that run-up.

The ref blows the whistle, but it's not for me to take the penalty. Instead, over to my left, United defender David May and Raducioiu are having a scrap on the edge of the box, and Peter Jones wants it to stop.

This is all I need! It's a bit of handbags really. There's nothing to it. I wipe my mouth with my shirt again, and try to stay focused while Raducioiu and May shake hands.

I'm ready to go now. I really am. If that whistle doesn't blow now, I'm going to fucking explode. My heart is pumping, I'm trying to stay focused. Come on, ref!

Peter Jones puts his whistle to his mouth and blows it. This is it.

•

I loved playing against Man United – they're some of the games that I still remember as if they were yesterday.

Any sportsman wants to test themselves against the very best and, in the era in which I played for West Ham in the nineties, there's no doubt that United were the best team in the country.

Their team was ridiculous – on that day in December 1996, Paul Scholes was on the bench, and Roy Keane was injured. Imagine having a midfielder of the calibre of Scholes on the bench! It's an absolute joke.

They had quality all over the pitch, but I loved the challenge. And the truth is, we'd always give that side a game at Upton Park.

Unfortunately, it was a different story at Old Trafford as we'd go there almost expecting to lose. I loved playing up there at that famous stadium, and I always gave my best, but in the back of your mind, you know you need a miracle to get any kind of result up there. That's not defeatist, just realistic.

Back at home, it was a different story, mainly because of our compact ground and the intimidating atmosphere created by the fans. You talk about a 12th man, and there were definitely times when the incredible Hammers support made a massive difference.

We had some great games against United, including a tight one in January 1996 when we trailed 1–0 to an early Cantona goal. I remember this one very well, not because we managed to win or even nick a draw, but because of an incident near the end.

I was trying to win the ball in my own half, under pressure from Andy Cole, and I slid in with two feet to keep possession, but Nicky Butt then chopped me down with a two-footed challenge of his own.

I shot straight back up to my feet as I'm not the kind of player to make a meal of a tough tackle, and instantly it felt like I had half of the United team looking for a fight.

Both Keane and Cantona got right in my face, with Eric even trying to punch me when the ref wasn't looking, as he was trying to find his red card to show to Butt, who was sent off for a second yellow.

The United players surrounded the ref Stephen Lodge, who started waving yellows to scare them off. Apparently, Keane was disappointed that I hadn't stood up for Butt, but I can't really believe that.

It's not like I lay on the pitch play-acting, I bounced straight back up. But he went in on me from behind, so there was not a great deal I could do, and I'm sure the ref had already made up his mind.

Keane was a fantastic player, who would walk into almost any side, but he would bitch and moan on the pitch more than any other player, especially when things weren't going his way.

I don't think he was such a tough player either. Yes, he could look after himself, but if you're going to fly around the pitch kicking people, you have to expect to be kicked back. You can't start moaning about it, as he often used to do, you just have to get on with it.

Keane was certainly moaning when we played at Old Trafford earlier that season. That was the day when Marco Boogers announced himself to the Premier League.

Apparently, Harry Redknapp had signed him without seeing him play, although he'd seen a video of him – but not on YouTube, this was the video tape variety. Marco had scored a shed load of goals in Holland so came to us with plenty of expectation.

He came off the bench in our first game of the season at Leeds, but didn't do a great deal. Like many of the foreign players at that time, the intensity of English football, both in matches and training, was a big shock to the system and took some getting used to.

However, none of us realised just how quickly Marco would settle in, as we found out at Old Trafford in our next game.

He came off the bench as we were trailing again, and seemed far more determined to make an impact, sprinting on to the pitch with purpose. United were playing keep ball, but Marco wasn't having any of it.

As the ball was moved across to Gary Neville on the right, Marco launched himself across the damp surface and slid for what seemed like about a minute, before absolutely wiping poor Gary out, with a knee-high challenge that even I have to concede might have been taking things a bit too far.

Neville collapsed in a heap and Steve Bruce came storming across to confront Marco, who looked well up for a scrap.

This was all taking place directly in front of me and as soon as I saw Bruce make his move, I steamed straight in there myself, as I had to defend my team-mate. It doesn't matter who they are, whether you get on with them off the pitch or not, in the heat of the battle, I would always live or die for anyone wearing claret and blue.

Bruce and Marco were busy exchanging shoves as I arrived, at almost exactly the same time as a very young David Beckham. I grabbed both of the United players, not because I was looking for a fight myself, but just to protect Marco from their anger. I had my arms around Bruce, and Beckham was sandwiched in between us.

At the same time, Peter Schmeichel joined the melee, launching a volley of abuse in Marco's direction. Nicky Butt then tried to pull me away from holding on to Beckham and Bruce, before a few others joined in for more pushing and shoving.

The only surprise was that Roy Keane wasn't involved. But there was no need for him to get in the ref's ear, because the red card was already out, to nobody's surprise.

Marco was handed a four-match ban for that challenge, and he never started a game for the Hammers, making two more sub appearances before a knee injury saw him return to Holland. Despite his short-lived time with us, the fans would never forget him purely for that moment of madness at Old Trafford.

And the players would never forget him either, as he almost got us into so many fights when we were out in the bars and clubs. Marco was a big bloke, over 6 ft tall, and just a bit clumsy with it. He had a terrible habit of stepping on other people's feet when we were out and about, and we often had to step in ourselves to make sure he didn't get himself into any trouble.

He'll forever be associated with that United game, and many of those Man United matches were memorable to me personally for so many reasons. But there's little doubt that some of my best career moments were scoring goals. For a full-back, I was lucky enough to score more than my fair share, and not just because I was the club's penalty-taker.

There were also free-kicks and plenty of others from open play because of the attacking way that I played the game. And there was nothing better than that feeling of seeing the ball hit the back of the net.

It was actually Lou Macari who was responsible for my goalscoring record, as when he took over from John Lyall, the man who signed me for the Hammers, he asked me to take the spot-kicks and free-kicks, and also encouraged me to get forward for corners, as he rated my aerial ability.

My trademark style was to absolutely leather the ball as hard as I could from the penalty spot. I strongly believe that a professional footballer should never miss the target from 12 yards, it's just not acceptable.

But I didn't always try to break the net with a thumping strike, as I toyed with placing the ball. It was a short-lived experiment. We were playing at Watford in a cup tie which went to penalties, and when I took mine I tried to place the ball to the keeper's left, and hit the post.

That was not a nice feeling, so I revised my approach and decided to go for pure power every time, no matter what. My theory was that if I hit the ball as hard as I possibly could and I didn't know which part of the goal it was going to end up in, then the goalkeeper certainly wouldn't know either. In general, it worked pretty well.

I remember missing a penalty against Sheffield United after that. I struck it very hard, but it cannoned back off the crossbar, and rebounded all the way to the outer edge of the centre circle! One of the Blades players picked the ball up, and they ended up winning a corner about five seconds after my spot-kick.

I missed another one when we were playing against Arsenal, but this one is far harder for me to recall. During the game, Ray Parlour managed to accidentally kick me in the head, leaving me with a concussion that I was only aware I had way after the game had ended.

I continued playing and took the penalty we won soon after, which apparently struck the woodwork. The problem is I have no recollection of any of that game, not immediately after it, and not even now.

And that's why when I went back into the dressing room at full-time, I innocently said to the kit man, 'We missed a penalty, didn't we?'

He replied, 'Yeah, you fucking did!'

That was certainly news to me at the time. The even crazier thing is that, being the times those were, I was allowed to drive home after the game, despite my total memory loss of the 90 minutes that I'd just played. Madness.

Luckily, I remember almost everything else about my career, especially the goals. Goalscoring came a great deal more naturally to me than the average full-back because I'd started life as a pro footballer as an inside-left at Birmingham, which meant I was used to playing further up the pitch, and no stranger to having a sight of goal.

Lou Macari recognised those instincts in me, and he'd stick around after training, laying the ball off to me to practise long-range shots, and I don't mean from the edge of the box. I'd be smashing them from 30-plus yards out with varying degrees of success, but it certainly helped me come match-day when I wouldn't be afraid to belt one from distance.

I also loved a goal celebration, but they would vary depending on the circumstances and sometimes who we were playing against. I once scored with my right foot against Bristol Rovers, and having grown up playing for Bristol City's age-group teams, that was quite a sweet moment. I loved that. Equally, scoring against my former club Birmingham was also great, even though I enjoyed my time there.

Probably the best free-kick I scored was against Nottingham Forest at the City Ground in a top of the table second tier clash. I stuck it straight in the top corner right in front of all our travelling supporters who had packed out the away end.

I once scored twice in a victory against Tottenham at Upton Park, and that was a great feeling as the fans loved beating Spurs.

Certainly, as I started scoring goals, alongside the combative nature of my game, there was more interest in me from the press, and from football in general. So when rumours began circling that Tottenham were interested in signing me, Lou was quick to act.

At that time, I was living in a place called Latchingdon which was about an hour's drive from Chadwell Heath. One afternoon, Lou called me up to say that he needed to talk to me because they'd had a bit of interest in me from Spurs.

It was about 4 p.m., so I got into the car and drove all the way in, through the rush hour traffic, and got to the training ground, where Lou was waiting for me.

I walked through the door into his office, and he says to me, 'You're not going!'

'You brought me all this fucking way to tell me that?' I replied.

'Yeah, you're not going!'

'You fucking wanker!' I yelled as I walked out of his office, got back into my car, and drove back home.

That was obviously Lou's way of letting me know that he was the gaffer, and I needed to listen to him, but I was far from happy at the time.

As it happened, I was more than happy to stay at West Ham. I loved the club, and the fans, and they seemed to love me, so why would I want to go anywhere else anyway? Especially when I was on penalties and free-kicks!

There was one game where I was on the receiving end of a penalty, however, when I famously pulled on the goalie's jersey in a match at Everton in 1995.

For all the spot-kicks I took, I can't say I ever thought for one second that I'd ever be standing on the goal-line trying to stop one going in. But that's exactly what happened at Goodison Park one night, when Ludek Miklosko was sent off for bringing down Daniel Amokachi in the box.

It was one of those very rare occasions when Harry Redknapp hadn't named Les Sealey on the bench, so there was no obvious replacement for the big Czech – and this was still before half-time.

All of us on the pitch were looking around at each other and it seemed obvious to me that nobody wanted to go in goal, so I thought to myself, 'Fuck it, I'll do it.'

There was no spare keeper's shirt so I had to put on Ludo's and, given that he was almost six-and-a-half feet tall, his jersey came down to my knees. Alongside that, I put on his gloves which were at least two inches too big. It may have been the Premier League, but standing there in Ludo's shirt and gloves, it might as well have been Sunday League.

My first job was to face the penalty which had been awarded for the foul on Amokachi and, fortunately, Tony Cottee gave me the inside track on David Unsworth's spot-kicks as TC had played at Everton for six years.

'He always puts them to the right of the keeper,' he told me as I tried to get my hands as far into my gloves as possible so the finger bits weren't flapping around in the evening breeze.

'Ok, got it, to the right,' I thought, although it would have been more natural for me to dive to my left as I'm left-footed.

Unsworth stepped up, and I kept my eye on him, although I put my weight on my right side, ready to leap that way. As he made contact with the ball, I launched myself to the right, and definitely had that side of the goal covered.

The only problem being that the ball sailed past me into the left of the goal, exactly where I would have been if Tony hadn't put doubt in my mind. Thanks a lot, TC!

That made it 2–0 to Everton, meaning it was now just a case of trying to keep it respectable. Coming from two goals down with ten men – and me in goal – was just never going to happen. To be fair, I did ok and made a few saves, although I fumbled a Graeme Stuart shot that could have gone in but for a last-ditch grab.

John Ebbrell made it three from a rebound after I'd saved a shot from Amokachi, but other than that, no further damage was inflicted.

The truth is I actually loved every minute of it. I played the rest of that game with a huge smile on my face. Maybe it was because the pressure was off, as there was little expectation on me, but having said that I wouldn't have wanted to be responsible for us getting an absolute hammering.

I was coming out and claiming corners in the air, even after Everton had brought on Duncan Ferguson, and I pulled off a few other half-decent saves. The travelling Hammers fans loved it, and they were singing *'England's number one'* at me and, even more incredibly, I was given the man of the match award.

Losing 3–0 is never nice, but in those circumstances I was quite pleased with my evening's work. But I certainly knew which side of the penalty spot I preferred to be on in the future – and I never listened to anything Tony Cottee said again!

•

Back to the penalty at Old Trafford, the whistle hasn't even finished being blown, and I'm on my way to strike that ball.

There are thousands of Hammers fans behind the goal,

all willing it to go in, but all paused in a moment in time as I run towards the ball.

I have my eyes only on the ball. There is no time in moments like this, just me and that ball, and the goalkeeper.

I want to see the ball hit the net. Right now, it's the only thing that matters.

I run until my right foot is planted on to the turf about a foot from the ball, and I swing my left boot back and then give it everything I've got to make the sweetest, yet most ferocious, contact with the ball that I possibly can.

And suddenly, before I can even blink, I see it rocket into the top left corner of the net, and I'm filled with an extraordinary feeling.

The noise is insane. I run to the side of the goal, right in front of the Bobby Moore Lower and the fans are going wild. Suddenly, as I stand there, some of the fans are alongside me on the pitch. The noise is deafening.

I can feel someone grabbing the back of my shirt, pulling me back. I think it's one of my team-mates, but the truth is I have no idea. Now, there is a pair of arms around my neck, hugging me.

Just for a few seconds, I am completely lost in this moment of ecstasy. I feel a pair of hands, one on each side of my head, covering my ears, and then a face that seems to belong to those hands plants a kiss right on my forehead.

It's bedlam. Absolute bedlam. And I love it. It's everything I ever dreamed of, and then some.

I don't know it now, but in a few years, Coca Cola will make an advert about this moment. It will feature a blind Hammers fan watching this game with his brother and his mate, and they're commentating to him about me putting the ball on the spot, and then there's a wild, enormous celebration in the stands as the ball goes in.

But that's in the future. Right now, stewards are trying to get the fans back into the stands, and suddenly I'm running back towards my own half. There's still plenty of time left in this game.

A few minutes ago, the game was lost, and I was more worried we might ship four or five goals, but now we're level. And who knows what might happen next?

I can hear 'You're not singing anymore' bellowing out around the ground as Man United prepare to kick off. Again.

The adrenaline is surging through my veins. We can win this game. I honestly believe we can do it.

The crowd are lifting us to new heights. They're making so much noise as we try to attack again. I smash a ball forwards, and eventually a shot comes in that's clawed away by Schmeichel for a corner.

I sprint to the penalty area. There's not long left, as Michael Hughes prepares to take the corner. I'm standing in the box, trying to make space for myself.

The atmosphere is loud again, brimming with expectation, as Michael plays the ball into the box. I watch it all the way and time my leap to perfection. Unfortunately, so does

Ronny Johnsen and I head the ball onto his head, and away it goes, the chance is gone.

As the crowd gasp in slight disappointment, expectation dashed, I groan inside. That could have been the winner.

But the ball is still alive. Hughes back-heels it past Giggs, and Dumitrescu has it on the edge of the box. I watch him shoot, and I'm willing it into the corner past Schmeichel, as is every single Hammers fan in the ground and watching on the box. But the big Dane stretches out his enormous frame and palms the ball away.

I'm back in my own half. There can't be long left. Once again I hear the ref's whistle, but there's no penalty being awarded. This time it is all over.

I shake Phil Neville's hand, then Ole Gunnar Solskjaer's. It's a blur of handshakes now, as the adrenaline starts to head out of my system.

We've drawn, but it feels like a win. As I leave the pitch, I know that my penalty is already a tiny part of West Ham history, and that's a wonderful feeling. Tonight, I'm a proud man.

THE PUB

Drinking Dicksy and the double double

I'm walking down Green Street, past all the stalls selling West Ham scarves, hats and badges.

It's Saturday, and it's about 1.30 p.m. Usually, I'd be heading into the stadium right about now to begin my pre-match warm-up.

But I'm not playing today, as I'm injured. In fact, I haven't played for a long time. Today, I'm a West Ham fan.

I continue past the greengrocers with the fruit and veg stands outside, and the old dears pulling their shopping trolleys along behind them, while their husbands head to the game.

Or maybe they're heading to Ken's for a fry-up. Or Nathan's for pie and mash. They could even be in the Boleyn, for a snifter or two before the game. That's where I'm heading.

There are thousands of people everywhere, and we're nowhere near kick-off time.

I go past the sports shop which is open. I think this is the one Bobby Moore used to own at one time, but I could be wrong. One of the lads told me that a while back.

I'm a face in a sea of people, so nobody stops me. Occasionally, I get a smile or a nod, or maybe a finger point at me, but I'm walking quickly, or at least as fast as my recovering knee will allow me.

I approach the corner of Upton Park, and there's an enormous queue right outside the Boleyn, the pub that stands right there next to the ground. Shit. I don't know if I'm even going to get in there now.

I get closer to the pub, and can see this queue is not actually going into it, it's going in the opposite direction.

I look towards the end of the queue in the distance, and realise that this is the queue for Nathan's. There must be about 150 people all waiting for their pie and mash.

I smile to myself, because I know from experience that it is definitely worth the wait, so good on 'em.

I open the pub door and the air is immediately thick with smoke, and the noisy buzz of thirsty football fans.

I can barely walk a step past the door as there are so many people in the pub. I can barely even see the bar. It must be about ten-deep in front of it.

Fuck me, I'm never getting a drink in here. I look around, as a couple of fans give me a nod, a back slap and an 'alright Dicksy!'

I'm surveying the scene, when suddenly someone grabs my arm, and I look to my right and they're putting a pint of lager in my hand.

'Cheers Dicksy!' says the voice belonging to the arm-grabbing, pint-putter-in-hand.

'Cheers!' I say raising my glass, but I can barely lift it to say cheers, let alone get it to my mouth to take a sip, because it's that rammed in here.

'How do you think we'll get on today?' he asks.

'I reckon we should win,' I reply, then manage to take a sip of the beer.

As I do that, a bloke in front of me hands someone at the back of the ten-deep bar a £20 note. I watch that £20 note being passed along to the bar and, eventually, five beers and some change make their way back, over everyone's heads.

By the time the pints arrive, they're probably only around three-quarters full, but the bloke doesn't seem to mind, as he hands them out to the people around him.

What a place this is! I'm loving it, and then another bloke comes over to me with two drinks in his hand, offering me one.

I still have my first drink in my hand, but I say thank you and take the bottle off him anyway.

'When you gonna be playing then?' he asks me.

'A month or two, hopefully,' I say.

'We need you back!'

'I need to be back, I'm desperate to play again.'

I finish my first drink, just about able to get the glass to my mouth, and then someone takes the empty out of my *hand, and it gets passed along the production line and back to the bar again.*

I carry on talking with a few fans, as somehow the place fills up even more. There must be about three or four hundred in here now, but I've no idea how that's even possible. It's nowhere near big enough.

But I'm loving the friendly atmosphere of the pub, and I'm getting as carried away as the fans, well up for today's game, like they all are.

I'm in the middle of a conversation with someone, and I can hear a few blokes start singing 'Bubbles' from the other end of the pub,

And now the whole pub is singing, me included.

'And like my dreams they fade and die . . .' we all chant together, pint glasses held aloft – for those who can get their arms in the air, and aren't restricted to keeping them by their sides.

'Fortunes always hiding, I've looked everywhere, I'm forever blowing bubbles, pretty bubbles in the air! United! United!'

Back to the football chat I go, and I feel like I want to get a round of drinks in myself but there is no way anyone here's going to let that happen.

So many people are offering me drinks, I'm now actually turning them down, which is a first for me.

It's also a first for me to be in the Boleyn on a matchday, but it definitely won't be the last time I do this. I'd love to come in here before a game even if I was playing.

If I could stay in here, having a drink with the fans until five to three, then run into the stadium to play, that's exactly what I would do. Not too sure that the gaffer would be happy with that though.

A few others start up 'Bubbles' again, and then we're all off, singing our hearts out. I look around the pub, and see all the faces. They're smiling as they sing, happy to be here, happy to be part of something.

And I realise I'm happy too. These are good, honest, hard-working people, who graft away during the week so that they can enjoy their football on a Saturday.

I'm missing my football so much at the moment, being a part of the squad, the banter in the changing room, all that kind of thing. But right now, I suddenly feel connected to all that again, thanks to this magnificent place.

I notice a bit more space appearing around me and look at my watch. It's 2.45 p.m. Time to go and watch the game.

I make my way back outside. The queue to Nathan's is nowhere near as big now, but there are still thousands of people everywhere, including loads still having a drink outside the pub.

Most people are heading into Upton Park now as it's so close to kick-off. It's like a sea of claret and blue, all marching together.

As I get into the ground, fans start a few chants as the atmosphere continues to build.

I'm lucky enough to go into the players' entrance today, even though I'm not actually playing. I say hello to the guy on the door – another friendly smiling face. They're everywhere today, I think, as I walk through to my seat in the stand, nodding, smiling and saying hello to plenty more friendly faces. Officials, families of my team-mates, even the odd steward I've got to know while I've been injured. Some of the people who make the club keep ticking behind the scenes, making it the great family club that it is.

I sit down and the place is already a cauldron of noise. I look over to the Chicken Run, where thousands have probably been in the ground for an hour already, trying to make sure they get the best spot to stand and watch the game.

There are kids perched with their legs dangling over the wall at the front, tucking into pies and chips.

And now a huge roar goes up all around me, ringing around the ground, as the teams make their way out on to the pitch.

When I'm playing, I hardly notice this as I walk out focused on the game, doing my job, giving everything for the cause.

Now, up here in the stands, it's amazing to be a part of this. I'm clapping the boys out, as 'Bubbles' starts playing over the tannoy, and suddenly we're all singing together again.

But now it's 25,000 voices together in the stadium, and the noise is mind-blowing. It's incredible.

There's nothing I want more than to be out there about to kick off and play for West Ham. But this is definitely the next best thing.

•

Ultimately, football is about the fans. It's not about anything else, no matter what some people would have you believe.

I always had a great relationship with the Hammers supporters from the moment I first pulled on a West Ham shirt. I'm sure the way I played the game had a huge amount to do with that, as I played in a way that made it obvious how committed I was, and I would never leave anything on the pitch.

Certainly when I started playing at Upton Park, football was a passionate, working man's game. Those blokes in the Boleyn and in the ground worked their bollocks off, and expected exactly the same from the players on their team on a Saturday afternoon.

That's why I was so concerned about the Chicken Run when I first signed for the club, as I hadn't enjoyed the experience of playing down that side of Upton Park with Birmingham. But once I was wearing a West Ham shirt, and showed the fans what I was all about, it was a very different story indeed.

You definitely wanted those fans on your side, rather than against you. And to make sure they were on your side, you had to love wearing the shirt, and you had to be prepared to give absolutely everything for the club. I'd like to think that I did both of those, every time I pulled on a claret and blue shirt.

Yes, I played very aggressively, but that was the game back then. It was a bit like kill or be killed out on the pitch sometimes.

Of course I played for myself, as I had to support my family, there's no denying that. But I also always played for the supporters. At the end of the day, they're paying your wages. All they want you to do is to give everything for that shirt, and I made sure I always did that, win, lose or draw.

When I think about West Ham now, I don't think about the players, the manager, or the club owners. I only ever think about the fans because they're the constant. They, or their families, have been coming for as long as any of them can remember. West Ham is in their DNA.

A while back, I was doing a supporters' Q&A at the club. I do a lot of those, because those events are all about the fans, and even though I don't play anymore, that relationship still exists, and it's one that I want to maintain as much as possible. That's why I've always been happy to do interviews for the fan sites, podcasts, and anything connected to West Ham really.

I always get asked what my favourite memories of Upton Park are, and I always say it's the supporters and that special atmosphere. Football is nothing without fans – look at those horrible games during the pandemic, when there were no fans in any of the stadia. It was absolutely awful and completely unwatchable.

At this Q&A, this lovely old dear and her old man came up to me for a chat. She told me that the poor bloke had terminal cancer. I looked at him, told him how sorry I was, and then also realised how much I recognised his face. He looked very familiar to me.

The old dear was clutching a photograph in her hand which she handed over to me. I had a look at it, and saw that it was a snap of me and her fella from about 30 years ago. He was one of those fans that I would see so often around Upton Park, he was almost part of the furniture.

I didn't remember getting that photo taken because there have been that many of them, but I did remember his face. She wanted me to have the picture so I kept it and I've still got it because, to me, this is what playing football for West Ham was all about. It was just a fantastic, community club. A place for family and friends to come together, and it meant everything to me that I was able to serve the club as I did.

When Billy Bonds was the gaffer, some bright spark who was running the club came up with the idea of a bond scheme, where supporters would be charged an absolute fortune for the privilege of being able to buy a season ticket. Effectively, they were trying to mug the fans of more of their hard-earned cash so they could continue to come and watch West Ham.

Understandably, the supporters were up in arms about the idea, and there were many protests, mostly outside the ground. However, during one home match, a young fan ran on the pitch, grabbed a corner flag, and sat with it in the centre circle in protest.

I totally sympathised with him, and the other fans, but ultimately we had a game of football to play, so myself and Martin Allen went over to him to try to diffuse the situation.

I managed to get the corner flag back, and we talked him down, before he was led off the pitch by stewards. During the stoppage, a few more fans came on and one ran towards me looking like he was going to kill me or something, but instead he came straight up to me and said, 'I fucking love you!'

'Oh cheers,' I replied.

After the game, I was asked about the incident by the press, and I didn't hold back. At the time, we were struggling quite badly and I was quoted in the papers as saying that you can't expect people to fork out that kind of money to watch a load of shit.

I think they were asking close to a grand for a seat which, at that time, was a hell of a lot of money. It was taking liberties with the fans, and there was no way I wasn't going to speak up for them. I didn't care about what I was supposed to say or not supposed to say as a player. It never entered my mind.

Unsurprisingly, it ended up costing me, because the club fined me two weeks' wages for speaking out like that. I know that Billy Bonds felt the same way I did, but he couldn't say anything about it because he was the manager, but I was very happy to have the opportunity to speak my mind, and stand up for the fans, who were the real owners of the club.

I can honestly say that if the situation had come up again, I would have said exactly what I thought in a heartbeat. How could I not back the fans when they always backed me? Even when I was getting red cards left, right and centre, they always stuck by me. When I was sent off at Derby, I think they were still singing my name even when I was walking down the tunnel. The majority of people in football haven't shown me anywhere near the same loyalty, so I really owed so much to the fans.

That's why I was never worried about going out to have a drink with some of my team-mates even after a game in which we'd got beat. Even when we lost, people still wanted to buy me a drink, which is nice.

You're always going to get a bit of stick, here and there, but that's just part of life as a footballer. By and large, in that period we went out in Romford, Barking, Ilford, wherever, and we'd let our hair down a bit after a game. We'd have a few drinks, smoke a few cigarettes, and none of the fans had any problem with it. As long as we came off the pitch knowing we'd given it everything we possibly could, then we felt comfortable going out after the game.

This was also a time before mobile phones with cameras or video on them, so there was never going to be anybody taking pictures of us, or anything daft like that. What's more, the fans felt a connection to us, because at that point we weren't earning millions. Ok, we were well paid for playing football, but not to today's levels, so when we went out, we'd be in the same pubs, bars and clubs as the supporters. I think that made a huge difference to how they perceived us.

The other thing about that era was that our club, and many others, had a strong drinking culture. Arsenal players may have had their Tuesday club where they all went out and got plastered, but we pretty much had the Saturday, Sunday, Monday, Tuesday and Wednesday clubs.

Even after an away game on a Saturday, we'd all have a few beers on the way back. It wasn't a case of falling off the coach as some of the players would have left cars at the training ground, or wherever the coach was dropping us off.

And some players were tee-total as well, but they were still very much included in whatever was going on. As long as there was something about you, it was fine.

Some players preferred to keep themselves to themselves, which was also respected. After every game, when Billy Bonds was still playing he'd go into the Players' Lounge, pick up four cans of light ale, get into his car and go home.

On the other hand, the Players' Lounge would be our first port of call after a game. Once we were done with the free booze in there, we'd move on to the pub, then go to a nightclub. There would usually be a group of eight or nine of us, and we always had a lot of fun.

The foreign players who played for West Ham in the nineties certainly changed things a bit. A lot of them smoked, but they weren't into their drinks the way most of us were. We welcomed them all with open arms, and I would have died for any of them on the pitch because they were my team-mates first and foremost. We had players like Ilie Dumitrescu, Paulo Futre, Florin Raducioiu, Dani, and Hugo Porfirio, and they were all great lads.

They'd often say, 'Let's go out for a meal together tonight,' and we'd say, 'No, no, no, no, we're going to a nightclub!'

We'd always invite everyone out for a drink, it certainly wasn't an exclusive club. And most of them would come with us and have a drink. But when I say a drink, that's exactly what I mean. They'd have a glass of wine. And alongside them sipping their wine, people like me, Razor Ruddock and John Moncur were necking 20 bottles of beer each. They were probably thinking, 'What the fuck kind of football club have I come into?' And who could blame them? But we all stuck together and that certainly helped with the team spirit, and we seemed to do a lot better at that point, avoiding any relegation struggles.

The big changes came with the way the overseas players ate, rather than how they drank (or didn't). It's well-documented how the influx of foreign footballers changed the eating habits of English players, and that was certainly the case at West Ham as players' diets started to be taken more seriously at that time – unless you were Razor Ruddock, of course, although he did put away a serious amount of food, in his defence.

There were no real problems with language either, as so many of them spoke decent English as a second language. We're quite ignorant as English people, when we go to other countries and play football and don't make any effort to speak the language. I remember that our Czech keeper Ludo Miklosko struggled in the beginning, so I made things very simple for him. I said, 'Ludo, every time you get the ball, fucking throw it to me!' and he must have understood what I meant, because I swear he did exactly that every single time he got the ball.

I also used his lack of English to have a bit of fun when we were out in the pub together. He paid for some drinks, and when he was given his change by the barman, I told the great big silverback of a goalie that it was polite to say, 'Fuck off.'

I'm sure Ludo knew what it meant as most people around the world seem to know that particular English phrase, but he still said it to the barman when he got his change back, and we obviously found that very funny. I don't think the poor bloke working in the pub was too impressed, but I apologised to him and explained it was just a bit of banter.

As much fun as it was going out after games, some of the best memories I have are of the drinking sessions that took place behind closed doors, like our hotel rooms before matches. That wasn't a regular occurrence – although I always had my Jack Daniel's with me whenever we went away – but sometimes it would just go wild, especially if we'd travelled far.

That was the case when we went to Italy to take on Cremonese in the Anglo-Italian Cup in 1992. Whatever you think of that competition, and I thought it was a load of shit, this was a particularly legendary trip, because of a game of Spoof we played.

For the Anglo-Italian away matches, you travelled the day before, stayed in a hotel, then flew home straight after the game. And it wasn't a case of rotating players either, as we had a small squad and we played Saturday, Tuesday, Saturday, Tuesday. So we always had to make sure we made the most of our night in the hotel. On this particular evening, I was sharing a room with Kenny Brown, while Ian Bishop and a team-mate were in another room, but they came into ours to play Spoof, the game where you each have three coins, and everyone has to guess how many of them are being held behind our backs.

There are no winners in this game, only a loser, and the loser has to have a drink from the minibar as a penalty. We'd make up some awful mixes for the loser, like a glass of whisky, gin and milk, for example. It was whatever came into our heads at that time, we'd just make it up on the spot.

After several rounds, we'd emptied our minibar, so Bish and his room-mate went to their room to get their stock. The game went on for a long time, and by 1 a.m., we were all extremely drunk and both minibars had been drunk dry.

Bish and his room-mate headed back to their room, except when the latter opened our door to get out, he just collapsed and hit the floor like a sack of shit, without even protecting himself with his hands. He was completely gone, and I'd never seen anybody do that before. It was quite shocking. And a tiny bit funny.

We picked him up and put him in his bed, making sure he was lying on his side, and not likely to puke or anything like that.

The next morning, the day of the Cremonese game, he looked a very sorry sight indeed and he kept well out of Billy Bonds' way all day in case the gaffer got wind of what had gone on.

But he couldn't avoid having to play in the game that night, which didn't go well for him. We got beat 2–0, but he got absolutely battered. Back then, the Italian sides were horrible and would elbow you, spit on you, and do whatever they wanted as the refs didn't take any notice.

He was already feeling awful, but the centre-backs hammered him, going through the back of him time and again. They absolutely obliterated him. I did feel for him, especially with how bad he must have been feeling, but it was also very amusing. Welcome to Italy, mate.

Another team-mate, Trevor Morley, got a bit of stick over the years. It was all over the papers that he'd been stabbed by his missus, and he'd been critically ill in hospital. We were all very concerned for him, and it was a relief to hear that he was recovering.

So the whole team made a pact that when Trevor came back into the club, no one would mention the stabbing, and we'd let him re-integrate back into the group as he must have been so shaken up.

At the time, I was having rehab for my knee injury so I was always in early, working my bollocks off to get fit. Trevor also had to come in for treatment to his wound, and to stay fit. But on this one morning, I was in first and locked the door to the treatment room.

I could hear a lot of people trying to get in, but I was too busy to take any notice of that. Inside the treatment room, the physio John Green had a stand-up skeleton that he would use to educate us about our injuries. I decided that it would be a bit of a laugh to stick about 20 knives into the skeleton, then I opened the door and let everyone in.

As Trevor came in, I said, 'Here you go, Trev, I thought I'd make you feel at home!'

Soon enough, Trevor was fit enough to return to the team, and at the first away game we all went to, I went down to dinner early. We always ate together as a squad, before heading off to our rooms, so before anyone else got down there, I went around the dining room, and removed every single knife from the dinner table. The lads absolutely loved it. So much for that pact.

That kind of banter was why I loved playing with those West Ham players so much. The other reason was the respect between players and fans. That connection between myself and the fans is still very much there.

The bottom line is that I've never felt a particular bond to the club itself – that might sound strange because, as I may have mentioned once or twice, I love West Ham. For me, it's always been about the fans, and it always will be.

•

I'm back on Green Street. I'm in the car, although it's not the Fiesta Popular Plus 1.1 that I used to drive up here.

My mind is racing as I slow down and survey the scene. I have a memory of Billy Bonds talking to me about how this road used to be full of East End barrow boys with the market in full swing, even on a matchday. Different times.

Back then, the players all lived locally, including Bobby Moore whose house wasn't far from the ground. You might see him picking up a paper in the newsagent. Imagine that!

I stop the car at a traffic light and look around me. More memories. Things had changed a bit by the time I joined the club, but the atmosphere was similar. It smelled of community, of a club that belonged to the locals.

I continue driving towards Upton Park. The road and the pavements are fairly quiet. It's not a matchday.

I've obviously been around here plenty of times before when there was no match on because we'd sometimes train here, or have to come into the club for other reasons.

Those were the days. The days of Nathan's on Barking Road after training. I can almost taste that wonderful pie and mash, as I think about it.

It was just behind the Bobby Moore Stand. It was a proper East End institution, owned by locals, who used to work there as well. My usual in there was always the 'double double' – two lots of pie, with loads of mash. Absolutely superb.

I'm imagining myself sitting in there with some of the lads right now, as I carry on driving slowly up towards the ground.

My mind continues to wander off, as I remember going into Ken's Cafe on Green Street for a full English after training occasionally. That was also somewhere the players would go together.

Depending on the day of the week, the other option after training was the Boleyn for a traditional lunch of crisps and lager.

After training, it certainly wouldn't be a case of ten-deep at the bar with cash being passed over heads, and three-quarters of a pint making it back into your hand. During the week, the Boleyn is a quiet place with a few old boys supping their pints, and nobody singing 'Bubbles'. I always find it hard to believe it's the same place as it is on a Saturday afternoon.

And now I pull up at the side of the road because I've arrived at the junction of Green Street and Barking Road, and I'm right in front of the Boleyn.

The memories come flooding back. I can almost hear the fans singing, all of us barely able to move in there. Everyone wearing claret and blue.

I have a strange sensation inside. Call it nostalgia, call it whatever you like, but I miss those days, and they seem a long time ago.

I'm sitting in the car with all these thoughts flowing through my head, and I decide I'm going to have a walk around. Why not? Let's see what Upton Park looks like now.

I park the car, and head off towards the stadium. There are some bubbles painted on a street wall, and a little Bobby Moore mural just next to them.

But, as I turn the corner into Castle Street, I'm greeted by the most unfamiliar sight, because where the stadium should be, there's now a huge property development. Upton Park is no more.

I know that, of course I know that. But yet it's still the strangest thing to see it with my own eyes. I'm looking at the place now where the stadium should be standing, and it's just not there.

I can feel my heart aching and longing to see this great, iconic, football arena. Instead, there are beige-brick blocks of flats all over the place, as far as my eyes can see.

But there are still some remnants. The Hammer Social Club sign still sits proudly on a wall in front of me. To my right, down an alley, is an eye-catching mural which reads 'Long Live the Boleyn' – I presume it's referring to the stadium rather than the pub.

I have the strangest sensation as I continue walking because it's suddenly so hard to get my bearings. The place that was home for so long, that I knew like the back of my hand, is no longer there, and I can barely work out where everything used to be.

I walk around the property development. They've done a decent job to be fair, as there are gardens everywhere, including a Boleyn Ground Memorial Garden that I notice.

I have so many special memories of the ground and the places that surrounded it. I was 19 when I first came here, back in the spring of 1988. It's a world away from where we are now.

But I'm happy I played in the era that I did, when I could play the way I did, when we could go out the way we did, when we could have a connection with the fans the way we did. I honestly don't think I'd have it any other way.

I'm walking back to the car now, back past the Boleyn pub, back past all those memories.

The truth is that I think about football every day. I think about West Ham and Upton Park every day, and I do try to come back here every six months if I can, even now when the ground is no longer here.

It's important for me to keep that connection with the area, as I can imagine all those people and places still being there. I get in the car, start the engine, and drive off, all these lovely thoughts and happy memories continuing to buzz around my head.

THE RED MIST

This express train is not stopping

I've got the ball at my feet, and I look up. I see Kevin Keen ahead of me and pump it forward about 40-odd yards.

I couldn't have hit it any better. Kevin has left Jason Kavanagh for dead, and he's bombing towards the box, as I keep running forwards myself.

I'm past the halfway line, as Kevin puts a cross in which eventually gets half-cleared, but Peter Butler is there to chip it back into the penalty area, where Trevor Morley knocks it into the net.

I'm near the box myself now, and suddenly there are loads of us surrounding Trevor, piling on top of him and each other.

Get in there! We're 2–0 up at Derby and we've only been playing 15 minutes. This is what it's all about, we're all buzzing. The travelling Hammers fans behind the goal are loving it too, enjoying a great away day.

I pat Trevor on the head, and then jog back to my own half, waiting for Derby to kick off again.

There's still so much time left in this game, so we've got

plenty of work to do. No room for complacency, even if we are cruising. That's exactly when things can go wrong.

But it won't make any difference to me though, as I play football the same way, whether I'm playing in a professional game on a Saturday, or keep-ball in training.

There is no chance that I will shirk any challenge, avoid any confrontation, or hold back in any way.

My aim is to be as competitive in the 90th minute, as the first, regardless of the score. That's how I play football, and it's how I've always played football. I genuinely don't know any other way.

The game's restarted, and I'm tracking my man, the Derby right-winger Ted McMinn. I keep my eyes firmly on him, and the ball. Who says men can't multitask?

But I'm not thinking about that, I'm totally focused on the game, and doing my job. I get forward as we launch another attack, but this one comes to nothing.

I'm back in my own half again. I don't stop running. It feels like I don't even stop moving at all, unless there's an injury or something like that.

Nobody will be getting past me today. If Ted tries to take me on, he knows what will happen. It won't end well.

Usually, the wingers I come up against are fast but small, so clattering into them and letting them know who's boss is a simple job.

But Ted McMinn is a different specimen. He's 6 ft tall, and a very physical player. That doesn't happen often.

Still, it's not going to change my approach. It just means my job of keeping him quiet is slightly harder than usual. But I'm up for that. I'm well up for that.

In fact, I'm probably too up for that as he tries to come past me with a dribble, but I take him out for the third or fourth time with a fairly hefty challenge, and this time the referee Alan Wilkie decides he's seen enough.

He takes my name, shows me a yellow card, but I'm not overly concerned. This happens fairly often.

On we go, and there's not a great deal happening. When you're 2–0 up away from home, the main priority is to protect that lead.

So we're slightly less of an attacking force now, but equally Derby aren't exactly creating many chances. They've got Paul Kitson up top, but we've managed to keep him quiet so far. And I'm doing my best to cut the supply line to him from the right.

Derby are building from the back, and the ball is played out to their right, our left. I'm watching like a hawk, as I'm sure their right-back is going to give it to McMinn.

As the right-back looks up, he's searching for McMinn, who's probably about 5 yards inside his own half.

I can see what the defender's going to do, and there's no way McMinn is going to receive that ball.

I start sprinting as the pass is made. I'm over the halfway line. McMinn is side-on to me, so he can see me coming from his right.

The ball is there. It's there to be won, and about 3 or 4 yards from making contact, I launch myself, and start to slide to where that ball will be in about half a second from now.

I'm flying along the ground, keeping my eye on that ball. There's absolutely no way he's getting it. It's my ball, I'm having it.

As I slide, I await the impact, almost relishing it. This is what I love. The heat of the battle. The desire. The will to win. I bloody love it.

McMinn just about gets to the ball before I make impact. But it's way too late for me to do anything about that now.

I slide right through him like an express train, but his one eye has seen me coming and he leaps up in the air, rides my challenge, before collapsing in a heap about 5 yards behind me.

My first concern is where the ball is, but it's ok, it's been cleared from danger and out of play.

I'm back on my feet, and the referee is walking towards me. Surely, he's not going to give me another yellow when I haven't touched the bloke. Maybe a warning, but nothing more than that.

McMinn is still on the deck, and I suddenly have a very uneasy feeling about this.

Wilkie is fumbling around in the chest pocket of his black shirt, and I'm staring at him. He's about 10 yards from where I'm standing, and doesn't come any further.

He looks down into his pocket to see which card his fingers are holding, and eventually he pulls out a card and waves it in the air at me – from 10 yards away.

It's red. It's fucking red. I don't believe it. A red for a mistimed tackle! I would have been gutted if I got a yellow for that. McMinn is still lying on the pitch, and now I'm utterly livid.

'You fucking prick!' I scream at him. 'You fucking prick!' I yell again, pointing at him.

I'm so angry, and the worst part is there's absolutely nothing I can do about this. This prick has got me sent off.

If he gets straight up, I probably wouldn't have even got booked. But instead, with my reputation and a player on the deck, I'm off.

I keep screaming at McMinn, and suddenly Clive Allen, my team-mate, has his arms on me and is trying to console me, while walking me off the pitch. I'm so close to the touchline and the dugout that it'll barely be a walk of shame.

Everyone's off the bench, and on the pitch. The gaffer Billy Bonds, the assistant Harry Redknapp, who has his arm around my shoulder. Even Derby's Martin Kuhl, my former Birmingham team-mate, is trying to calm me down, but I'm still steaming.

'You fucking prick!' I yell again, trying to make myself heard over all the arms and calming voices surrounding me.

Suddenly, I find myself walking across the touchline, back

towards the players' tunnel. Harry's arm has been replaced by our kit man's, Eddie Gillam.

Good old Eddie. He's a top man. But right now, I don't want him or anyone else around me, as I trudge down the tunnel and back to the away dressing room.

I know that he's only doing his job, as he has to make sure I'm ok, but this isn't the first time poor Eddie has had to accompany me back to the dressing room. We've been here before.

It's only 3.30 p.m., I shouldn't even be coming back here for another 15 minutes, and yet here I am. My afternoon is over.

I train like a dog all week for this, and I didn't even make it through the first half.

Eddie doesn't say a word as we continue to walk down the tunnel that I was stood in half-an-hour ago, ready to play, ready to give it everything. Well, I certainly did that, I think to myself.

He holds the changing room door open for me, and I walk in there and sit myself down on one of the benches.

I put my head in my hands. I can see the tackle replaying in my mind. I definitely didn't make contact with McMinn. I know I didn't. Yet, I'm now off the pitch.

Worse than that, I start to worry that I'm going to cost us points. We were cruising at 2–0, but now we might be right up against it for the remaining hour of the game.

I pray that I don't hear a huge cheer from the stands above me, because that would clearly be a Derby goal. But it stays relatively quiet.

'You ok?' I hear Eddie say.

I look up and he's standing by the door, trying not to bother me, but also doing his job at the same time.

'Yeah,' I say, although I certainly don't feel like that's the case. I'm still angry, and pissed off.

Eddie's still staring at me. He has to stay with me until he's sure I'm not going to do something stupid like trash the place. He might have a long wait.

'Was that a definite red card?' I ask him.

'It wasn't a great challenge,' he says, confirming my worst fears.

'I never touched him, Eddie, god's honest. He jumped over me!'

'Yeah, well it didn't look good,' he says.

I'm sure he's probably right about that. I feel ever so slightly calmer, but still very annoyed about the whole situation.

'Look, I'm ok,' I say, meaning he can go now.

He heads back to the dugout to watch the game, while I carry on sitting here feeling sorry for myself.

I have a quick shower and get changed, by which time the boys are back in for half-time. I don't say much.

I know the gaffer's going to give me a bollocking. This isn't the first time I've been sent off this season. In fact, it's the third. Three red cards and it's only January.

It doesn't look good. The gaffer's going to have a pop at me, but I always give as good as I get from Billy.

But it's only half-time, so the focus is on holding on to our lead in the second half. The bollocking will wait until later, although he does find a second to call me an idiot for getting sent off.

As everyone heads back out on the pitch, I decide to go with them. Not on the pitch, that wouldn't go down well, but to the dugout.

Technically, you're not allowed to do that, you have to go into the stands or maybe watch from the tunnel, but I feel like taking a seat on the bench, so I do.

I'm still feeling a bit rebellious because I shouldn't have been sent off. As long as Wilkie doesn't spot me, I'll be fine.

I know I've left the boys in the lurch a bit, so I really want them to hold on and win the game. Or else I'll feel even worse.

That's my biggest fear with getting sent off – letting down my team-mates and the fans.

Hand on heart, I can always say that I give everything I could possibly give on the pitch. Yes, I have bad games, and I make mistakes. And sometimes I get sent off, but no one can ever question my passion and pride for my club.

That's what I'm thinking as I sit on the bench, watching the boys working hard for the three points. I'm trying to justify my red card to myself. I suppose what I'm saying is that it comes with the territory.

I can't be that blood and thunder, passion and pride type of player, and not pick up the occasional red card.

Except three in half a season is a little bit more than occasional. Maybe I need to be a bit cleverer, as I'm now clearly a marked man.

When a referee sees a player collapse in a heap near me, I'm far more likely to get a card because of my reputation.

I'm sitting here at the Baseball Ground with all these thoughts flying through my head, and the game in which I should be playing, carrying on in front of me, without me.

To be perfectly honest, it's not a great feeling.

•

I remember that January day in 1993 so clearly. The Ted McMinn red card turned out to be the penultimate sending-off of my career, my eighth in total.

Every red I got, would be followed by a period of me feeling sorry for myself and beating myself up, but I clearly didn't beat myself up enough as I ended up getting sent off nine times.

In a way, I'm happy that none of those red cards were for dissent to the referee or anything stupid like that. I can always hold my head up high, knowing that every single one was a direct result of my physical commitment to the cause.

I've always played football the same way, since I was a kid. I'm not saying I got nine red cards when I was a child, but when I was playing at school or for West Town Harriers in Bristol, I always gave it everything I could.

My first sending off came when I was playing for Birmingham's youth team against West Brom. I was 16 at the time, and flew into a couple of tackles that the referee didn't like so he showed me his red card.

I couldn't believe it. I felt like absolute shit, and the youth team gaffer didn't hold back either, reading me the riot act in the dressing room. I came out of there with a face like thunder, and started to head off for the team bus.

But before I could make it out of the ground, I was stopped by a very familiar-looking figure. He was only 5 ft 3 tall, or should I say short, one of his eyes was kind of elsewhere, and he didn't have much hair.

It was England World Cup winner Nobby Stiles, who was managing the Baggies youth side at the time.

'Look son,' he said, 'That ain't gonna be the only time you're gonna be sent off!'

I smiled at him, and he had a cheeky grin on his face. I immediately felt so much better. Here was an English football legend, who happened to be a very aggressive ball winner in his day, giving me some words of comfort and reassurance at a time when I needed them most. It made a huge impression and it was something I carried with me throughout my career.

I'm not sure how much it helped me a few years later, however, when I got my first red as a professional player.

That was during an infamously wild game against Wimbledon in the League Cup in 1989. One of the journalists reporting that night called it a disgrace to football, although I'm not too sure about that myself.

That Wimbledon side were well-known for being very physical but I didn't mind that at all. This was football, and that's how the game should be played – physically. You also have to remember that this was 1989. All games were physical then in a way that would be completely unacceptable now. Every game would be abandoned now if they were played like we did back then because there wouldn't be enough players left on the pitch.

Games against that Wimbledon Crazy Gang team were always dirty. They had Vinnie Jones, whose reputation was fairly similar to mine, and Dennis Wise, who was a horrible little fucker to play against. We used to kick the shit out of each other every time we stepped onto the pitch, but I had absolutely no problem with Dennis. He gave as good as he got, and after every game we'd shake hands and have a drink in the players' lounge.

And that night at Upton Park was no exception. Dennis went in on me two-footed, and all hell broke loose as pretty much every player on the pitch became involved in a mass brawl. Personally, I thought it was a harsh challenge but just a part of the game. There was no need for the fighting which it provoked.

I got my marching orders in the second half after one

crunching tackle that didn't make contact with the ball too many for the ref's liking. It was an unusual one in that I didn't often get sent off at home – I was far more likely to be dismissed at hostile away grounds where decisions tend to go for the home team.

But we ended up winning the game, so I didn't feel too bad about the red card in the end. And remembering what Nobby Stiles had said to me was also a massive help. He was damn right too, as red cards continued to be waved in my direction with increasing frequency over the next few seasons.

But it was in that 1992/93 campaign that it all started to catch up with me, and really have an impact; when I picked up that third red against Derby, in just 24 games played.

The season hadn't started particularly well for me, and that was before a ball had even been kicked. I got back from holiday on the same day that pre-season training started, which was a mistake on my part, but I called the training ground as soon as I realised my error.

These were the days before mobile phones, so I had to rely on whoever answered the phone at Chadwell Heath. I rang the club to make sure Billy Bonds was told that I'd only just got back from holiday and would be back in for training the following day. I don't think that was asking too much, but the message was not passed on.

So, later that day, I received a phone call from Billy who wanted to know why I hadn't been at training. The person

I told insisted he didn't remember speaking to me. I wasn't best pleased with him to say the least, and I never quite forgave him for that.

So pre-season didn't get off to a great start for me, and nor did the season itself when we went to Newcastle for our third game of the campaign. That was probably the most inexplicable red card of my career as far as I was concerned. It was the only one that wasn't for a tackle, and to this day I still have no idea what caused me to elbow poor Franz Carr.

Franz was a decent player. A tricky, speedy winger, with plenty of skill. But he wasn't a particularly physical player who would kick you. He was actually a really positive player, who'd knock the ball past you and run. I could never catch him. Over 10 yards, he could give me a 5 yard head start, and he'd still beat me to the ball. He was genuinely rapid.

At St James' Park that day, I remember having the ball, and facing my own goal. I could hear him coming up behind me, and I just knew that I was going to elbow him. I knew it, but yet I couldn't stop myself. I have no idea what came over me.

As soon as he was close enough, I threw out my elbow into his face and he hit the floor like a sack of shit. It all happened so quickly. From the thought process to the act, to Franz hitting the floor. I didn't even bother waiting for the referee, because as soon as I'd done it, I just started walking towards the tunnel, because my afternoon in the northeast was over.

There was no need for Eddie Gillam to spend too much time with me, nor for me to ask him if he thought I deserved to be sent off. I spent about 10 minutes wallowing in self-pity for being so stupid, and not being able to control myself, then I got changed and watched the rest of the game from the tunnel. But I was full of regret, because a blatant elbow like that was not something that I'd ever done before.

My mind just went blank, as it did when Billy Bonds started laying into me after the game. It was a bollocking that was completely deserved, but I was never one of those players who accepts a dressing down like that.

I didn't really have a leg to stand on this time though so I just told Bill to fuck off and leave me alone. The truth was I just wanted to be left alone at that point because I was angry with myself, and I knew how stupid and unacceptable what I'd done was.

A few weeks later, Wolves away was a different story altogether, although the ending was the same as I saw red again. That sending-off was probably even more stupid than the one at Newcastle, purely in terms of my belief that there is no way I should have been dismissed.

Myself and Paul Birch were tussling for the ball. I had it and he was trying, unsuccessfully, to get it off me. To be fair, I had to twist and turn to try to shake him off and eventually he dived in at me and gave me a bit of a kick, so I did the same back to him, before trying to clear the ball. No major harm done there.

But from nowhere, Steve Bull came charging at me so I just kind of helped him on his way past me, and he ended up on the floor clutching his stomach as if I'd shot him. As if that wasn't mad enough, Birch then came flying in at me so I grabbed him by the neck and threw him to the ground too, where he ended up next to his team-mate, also pretending he'd been the victim of a knife attack.

The pair of them had gone down like babies, and hammed up the extent of it like a proper pair of play-acting pricks, in a clear attempt at getting me sent off. The problem for me was that it worked a treat.

While all that was going on, Billy Bonds had run down the touchline – I'd like to think he was coming to help me out by evening up the numbers, but he was actually coming to restrain me, with the linesman also somehow involved in the melee. It wasn't a great look, and it wasn't long before I was heading to the Molineux dressing room.

This time, the gaffer decided that a bollocking wasn't going to be enough. Billy decided that I was no longer fit to be captain of West Ham, and he took the armband from me.

Billy told me that as the captain, I was a player that people looked up to and respected, and the red cards were setting a bad example. He wanted to take that responsibility off me to calm me down, and try to get me to take some responsibility for my actions on the pitch.

As much as I loved being captain of West Ham – and I really did, it was a huge honour for me – the most important thing for me was playing football. So losing the captaincy didn't really bother me that much. Once I'd served my suspension, I was straight back in there, playing exactly the same way as I always had. Losing the armband didn't stop me getting stuck in, being aggressive, or even getting sent off again. I think Billy was trying to make an example of me to show the other players what he expected, but I'm not sure it made any difference to my game.

The fact is, if I had calmed down and lost some of that aggression then I wouldn't have been the same player. The irony is that Billy's decision probably made me even angrier.

Certainly, the events at the Baseball Ground a couple of months later showed that not a great deal had changed. Ultimately, I was always going to play the same way no matter what the match, and that even led me to get myself into trouble during friendlies.

During a testimonial against Tottenham, I got into a bit of a spat with Paul Allen. He may have been a former Hammer, but he was a feisty little fucker as well. We kicked each other, and I had the ball in my hand so I threw it in his face.

The ref gave our manager a simple choice – either I was to be subbed off, or I would be sent off. The substitution was duly made.

A similar thing happened in another testimonial game against Leyton Orient when I smashed into Warren Hackett. We squared up, and the referee suggested we both get subbed.

Neither of those came even close to what happened at my own testimonial when West Ham took on Athletic Bilbao at Upton Park in August 2000. I'd already retired at that point and my knee problem meant I could only play a small part in the game, so I wasn't on the pitch when it all kicked off.

It started when Nigel Winterburn smashed into Joseba Etxeberria and sent him right over the ad boards. That certainly raised the stakes a little, and then a few minutes later Igor Stimac clattered into Ismael Urzaiz, starting a 17-man brawl.

Paolo Di Canio was right in the thick of it, slapping some of the Spanish players, and when the police – yes, the police – and the ref had restored order, Paolo and Etxeberria had to be subbed off.

I was in the dressing room, when Paolo appeared. 'Julian, I'm very sorry I've been sent off,' he said.

'Mate, it's fucking fantastic! It's my testimonial, I really don't care!' I replied.

Paolo was a bit gutted about it, but I thought it was a very fitting way to send me off, so to speak. I got on very well with Paolo, and even after he retired and got into management, I used to play charity games with him.

He was obviously a very good player, but he certainly had his flaws, and not just because he shoved a referee over. I think a lot of what Paolo did was all for show, but he didn't produce enough magic on a regular basis. On his day, he was absolutely magnificent, but I felt that his days were too few and far between.

Before he moved to West Ham, we'd been on opposite sides when he was playing for Sheffield Wednesday, and I might have given him a slap during the game. Ok, I slapped him.

So when he arrived at Chadwell Heath, he said to Harry Redknapp, 'Julian is bad, he slapped me!' but the gaffer told him not to worry about me now that we were on the same team.

I'll never forget getting in the showers alongside him for the first time, and seeing that he didn't have a single hair on his body. I almost got a fright.

'Paolo, what the fuck are you doing?' I said.

'I shave my body,' he told me.

That was a new one for me, at the time. I was a man's man, and had never seen another bloke's body look like that so I found it very strange. The times were certainly changing.

Paolo was always very well-dressed, even for training. We would often wear suits before matches, but Paolo took the fashion stakes to a ridiculous level, turning up at training in really smart gear, straight off the catwalks of Milan and wherever else.

That was just how he was. The problem for him was that anyone dressing like that would always get their clothes hidden or chucked in the shower. That's just how we were. So, Paolo would often spend time screaming and shouting in the dressing room, demanding to know where his clothes were.

That was towards the end of my time at West Ham, but back in 1992/93, despite it not being the best season personally from a disciplinary point of view, it was a really memorable one for me as we got promoted to the Premier League for the first time.

I also scored 11 goals in the 34 games I played, which was a decent return considering I was a left-back. Only Clive Allen and Trevor Morley scored more goals than me so I was chuffed about that.

I was also pleased for Billy that he managed to get us up, as he's a West Ham icon who was adored by the fans. We may not have seen eye to eye on everything, but he deserved his success. And it was a fitting tribute to him that he should be the man to steer us back into the top flight.

I'll never forget the final day of that season. It was a tense one as we went into it needing to beat Cambridge at home to secure second place behind Newcastle. Any slip-ups, and Portsmouth were waiting to pounce.

Upton Park was absolutely buzzing, with more than 27,000 fans crammed in, willing us to victory. There were thousands outside the ground too, unable to get in as the place just couldn't hold any more people.

'Come on you Irons!' was bellowing out as the fans did everything they could to help after a goalless first half. The heat was on, we had to get the win in the second half.

I won a header from a corner which fell to David Speedie, who hooked it into the net. We were on our way.

Right at the end, Martin Allen played me in with a lovely, chipped pass which I ran on to, beat the defender, and was then facing the Cambridge keeper John Filan in a one-on-one, with Clive Allen on his own waiting for a tap-in, about 5 yards away from me.

It was one of those moments where I had a split second to weigh it up. Become a hero by scoring the goal that seals our promotion, or risk being the bloke that messed up getting the party started?

I squared it to Clive, who put it in the empty net and the place went absolutely wild. All the fans were straight on the pitch, mobbing us in the most ecstatic pitch invasion I've ever seen. 'I'm Forever Blowing Bubbles' rang out around the ground, as we were carried off the pitch on the shoulders of the fans.

In the dressing room, we clutched bottles of champagne and carried on singing, before going upstairs to the top tier of the stand, so we could be serenaded by the fans who were still on the pitch.

The most almighty East End knees-up was already up and running, creating special memories for everyone.

It was moments like that which will always stay with me, but if I'm honest, I know I'll probably be remembered for the other side of my game. Weirdly, it wasn't even a red card that caused what was probably the most controversial moment of my playing career.

In September 1995, we were playing Chelsea at Upton Park, a tough game against a side with Ruud Gullit running the show in midfield. But I approached it as I would any other, with my typical aggressive approach.

In the first half, John Spencer had the ball just outside the box on the right-hand side, and I attempted to jostle him away from the danger area. Without doubt, I fouled him, and he went down, and in my attempt to leap over him, I must have accidentally caught him on the head with one of my boots. Honestly, at the time, I wasn't even aware that had happened.

In fact, the moment I realised that I'd made that contact with him, was when John returned to the pitch with his head bandaged.

'Did you mean it?' he said to me, as he ran back on.

'Mean what?' I replied, genuinely not having any idea what he was on about.

'I've got eight stitches in my head!' he said.

'John, if I would've meant it, you'd have had fucking 28, not eight! I promise you I didn't mean it.'

He believed me, and stayed with that belief throughout the entire circus that followed.

A few minutes before the incident, he had tried to go through me, and many people have asked me if I was trying to take revenge. But as I've said many times, it's never really bothered me when people try to do that, I always saw it as part of the game.

To this day, I will always swear blind that I never meant to stamp on his head. It was a complete freak of an accident.

But the problem for me was that even though John Spencer believed me, Andy Gray on Sky Sports did not. The game was shown live on Sky's *Monday Night Football*, which meant Sky had more cameras than ever before at Upton Park so that Andy could analyse the game in the studio afterwards.

So he went through every angle of the incident after the game, time and time again. He must have shown it close to a hundred times.

What's more, he made his feelings very clear about it. I was guilty, so anyone watching would have been in no doubt about that.

When I went into training, Harry Redknapp pulled me to one side and asked me if I'd done it on purpose.

'No H, I didn't,' I told him.

'You fucking liar!' was his response, which left me in no doubt about what he thought. And he was my own manager!

The following Saturday, we went to Highbury to play Arsenal with the incident still fresh in everyone's minds, probably too fresh. I played the way I always did as I certainly wasn't going to play any differently as a result of what had happened the previous Monday evening.

I was booked in the first half by my old mate Alan Wilkie for a challenge on Glenn Helder. I thought it was a ridiculous decision as Glenn threw himself to the ground when I'd barely made contact. I wasn't happy, and made it very clear to both Glenn and Alan how I felt.

Then, I got both Ian Wright and a bit of the ball in the penalty area, and Wilkie pointed to the spot, but didn't show me a second yellow. Fortunately, Wrighty missed the spot-kick so I was somewhat relieved when we went into the dressing room.

Harry wasn't happy and warned me to calm down as we couldn't afford to go down to 10 men at Highbury. Despite his warning, I only had one way of playing so when I launched into a tackle on Wright 10 minutes into the second half, even though I'd made contact with the ball, the Arsenal man was writhing around on the floor like he'd been shot and Wilkie showed me my first red card since he'd sent me off at Derby.

Harry was fuming at full-time, telling me I'd let the team down, but that was nothing compared to what was to come. About an hour later, the MP David Mellor, a Chelsea fan who presented a football phone-in on Radio 5 Live, said the following on national radio: 'This animal has been sent off today and should have been sent off in the week.'

So I was an animal? Really? And he was allowed to say this to the nation, without giving me a chance to defend myself. Not just that, but the phone-in then featured a pile-on with everyone ringing in to put the boot in, encouraged by Mellor.

His relentless campaign against me was completely ridiculous, and I threatened to sue him. From nowhere, Nottingham Forest manager Brian Clough said that if I was going to sue Mellor, then he would sue me! Things were getting way out of control, to say the least.

My agent Rachel Anderson was doing everything she could to keep the press off my back at this time. She was the first female agent in football, and had been an enormous help to me, especially when it came to stuff like this. My wife at the time used to go to the gym with Rachel, and they had got chatting. Eventually, she became my agent, primarily to help me deal with the fallout from some of my red cards and problems with the football authorities.

I think she did a fantastic job, and I suspect part of the reason for that was that she was able to get away with a lot more than any male agent might have done. I used to do all the contract negotiations myself when I first started playing so I was less bothered about that side of things. I couldn't talk to some of the media who were giving me so much stick so that's where Rachel really came into her own.

She certainly had her work cut out at the time of that John Spencer saga, and the David Mellor nonsense was nowhere near the end of it.

Because of his role in replaying the incident on Sky, Andy Gray became a controversial figure for West Ham fans, but one fan went too far when a £10,000 price was put on the head of the Sky Sports presenter – I may well have done it myself for that money! – and Andy had to hire security during that time as the threat was taken so seriously.

Even more incredibly, my seven-year-old twin daughters got loads of abuse at school from Chelsea fans. They were being horribly bullied, all because of this incident on a football pitch, so I let the school have it, instantly took the girls out of there, and they had to be home-schooled for a while.

At that point, we asked a solicitor to write a letter to the media, asking them to lay off writing about me, as it was clear that this was now getting out of hand, with my children involved.

It's hard to believe the extent of the fallout from me accidentally treading on John Spencer's head. Unbelievably, the only person who had my back was John Spencer himself. He offered to defend me when I had to attend an FA hearing because they'd slapped a disrepute charge on me. But I was told his manager Glenn Hoddle stopped him from doing that, because he didn't believe me either.

At the FA hearing into the incident, I had a freeze-frame expert who proved that there was no way in the world I could have avoided making contact with John, so it was clearly an accident.

I saw the referee Robbie Hart there and he told me that he hoped I'd get off the charge, which was laughable because it was him who told the FA I had a case to answer in the first place.

'I wouldn't be here if it wasn't for you, you prick!'

In the end, it didn't matter what the ref or the freeze-frame expert thought, the FA threw the book at me anyway and I was banned for three games and fined £1800.

Neither of those punishments particularly bothered me, but I was livid that I'd been found guilty of doing something that I, 100 per cent, did not intend to do. And it still annoys me that to this day, football fans ask me about it, and laugh when I tell them it was an accident.

My agent tried to set up a meeting with Andy Gray because I wanted to find out why he was getting on my case so much. Unbelievably, he wouldn't agree to that. Instead, he invited me on to the show on Sky Sports, but there was no way I was going to walk into an ambush from him and all his mates at Sky.

A while later, we ended up meeting at some football dinner or other, and we spoke about the John Spencer incident.

'I didn't want you to have to go in front of the FA,' he insisted.

'So why the fuck did you keep replaying the incident?' I replied.

'It wasn't me,' was the general gist of his response, blaming the people behind the scenes at Sky.

I told him he was a fucking prick and walked off. I was absolutely certain that if it wasn't for him showing it over and over, even getting people to call in about it, the whole saga would never have blown up the way it did. And I would never have got that FA charge either.

The way it all played out was totally nuts. Things happen on the football pitch, and that's where they should stay. I also believe that I was a victim of my own reputation. When Roy Keane smashed into Alf Inge Haaland, nothing happened. No Andy Gray crusade on Sky, no David Mellor phone-in on the radio, and certainly no FA charge. And that challenge was far worse than anything I ever did throughout my playing career. I think the problem for me was that Roy was a Manchester United player, and I played for West Ham.

If Vinnie Jones had been involved in that John Spencer incident he would've had the same trouble that I did, because he was a Wimbledon player. I wasn't from a certain club, so I didn't have any extra protection and, as a result, I was thrown to the lions.

There were times when, believe it or not, the refs did take my side – even with my reputation. There was one game against Arsenal at Upton Park where I was having a running battle with Perry Groves, except it was a bit of a one-sided battle. He was playing on the right for the Gunners that day, which meant wherever he went on the pitch, I was right there, close enough to breathe all over him.

And that also meant I was close enough to nail him every time he got the ball. I won every tackle and header and, in the process, may have also come into contact with Perry once or twice.

He was far from happy. In fact, he was livid, as he felt I was kicking him all over Upton Park, and the referee wasn't doing anything about it. At one point, he went over to the ref, and said, 'Are you going to protect me?' and the referee replied, 'Why don't you go and play on the other wing?' which I thought was hilarious.

Perry actually started to walk over there but the Arsenal manager George Graham called him back. After another tough challenge, he berated the ref again: 'Aren't you going to send him off?' to which the ref responded, 'Not at Upton Park, I'm not!'

Eventually, Perry got subbed to spare him from any more suffering – although not before he'd done his best to try to get me dismissed. I did pick up a yellow card, but that was all on that occasion.

Apparently, my mum was far from happy with Perry's performance and pathetic attempts to get me in trouble, and she made sure everyone in the Upper Tier of the West Stand knew. She was so incensed that, after the game, she placed herself by the door of the players' bar, waiting for Perry to come for a drink after the game.

Fortunately for Mr Groves, he decided to swerve the post-match pint and get out of Upton Park. I don't really blame him for doing that. It was an intimidating place, and the crowd would definitely influence the referee. But back then the refs also had a bit of bollocks about them. Football's a passionate game. We would all swear and have a go at the ref if we felt decisions weren't going our way.

Back then, the likes of Keith Hackett, Clive Thomas and Roger Milford gave as good as they got. If I told them that I thought they'd made a shit decision, they'd come back with 'Leave me alone!'

It sounds weird, but there was a mutual respect where we both understood we had jobs to do. Nowadays, you can't even speak to a ref without getting booked or sent off. I honestly think that the referees believe they're the focal point of the game now which is so wrong.

When I was playing, even though I got red-carded many times, and booked even more, I could still get away with a few fouls before action would be taken. There's a video on YouTube of a moment from an FA Cup replay when West Ham played Sunderland.

A high ball came over and I went to meet it with my foot high and my studs up. I made contact with the ball to clear it into touch, but then in my follow-through, I smashed my foot straight into David Rush's chest, sending him flying off the pitch with the ball.

To his credit, he got straight up and didn't make anything of it, although he did have a word with the ref to show him that I'd made contact with his chest. The referee just told him to get on with it. Today, I'd probably get a 10-game ban for that kind of challenge.

•

Back at the Baseball Ground, I'm still stewing about my red card. Fortunately, the boys are doing a great job without me, and holding Derby at arm's length.

We're still coasting at 2–0, so it looks like I might get away with this one. Well, sort of. My main concern is that I cost us points, so hopefully we'll be ok now as there are only a few minutes left.

But, the gaffer will hit the roof at some point. I've already had the captaincy taken away from me after I was sent off against Wolves, so what will happen now?

He can't drop me, at least I know that for certain because this team needs me. But what if they decide to move me on and replace me with someone else?

I know that Harry is no fan of mine so he may well convince Billy that I'm not worth the trouble.

The thought of leaving West Ham is a horrible one for me, especially as I sit here on the bench watching the lads – this is what it's like to not be involved and I hate it.

My head's in my hands right now. I have to admit that I don't feel great about this.

I just can't seem to get out of this situation where every challenge I make is potentially a yellow or red card. It's like I'm being watched over more than any other player.

But is it my fault? Is it my fault that Ted McMinn jumped over my challenge and then over-reacted? Maybe it's my fault that I steamed in like a derailed high-speed train, but that's my game.

And that's the problem here – I'm always going to play the way I play. They can fine me, take away the captain's armband, hang me out to dry in the press, it won't make any difference.

I look up to see what's going on in the game. And as I do, the ref blows the full-time whistle and we've got the three points that we badly needed against one of our promotion rivals.

Thank god for that.

THE KNEE

A cab ride from Billericay.
And the fat lady clears her throat

'You c**t!' I shout.

'You absolute c**t!' I yell again.

This is all I can do to cope with this unbearable pain.
Fuck me, I don't think I can take much more of this.

I look to my right and John Green, the West Ham physio,
is grinning at me. He's also got his hands on my leg, just under
my knee, the source of all my swearing and agony.

I don't smile back. I can't smile back. All my energy right
now is focused on getting through this session, and getting the
fuck out of here, because I'm hating every second of it.

John looks at me. His hands are still just below my knee.
I know what's coming.

'Ready?' he asks, although why he asks is beyond me
because he's going to do it anyway, however I respond.

'No, fuck off!' I hear myself saying.

He laughs, then pushes his hands against my leg, just
bending my knee ever so slightly. Fucking hell, that hurts so
much. I feel like the whole thing's going to snap right off. I call
him a c**t again. Loudly.

The knee is so stiff, it needs to be bent manually. I can't do it myself so John is doing the honours for me.

We've been doing this for what feels like years, but is probably weeks or months. Each time, it bends a bit more, and I'm a step closer to playing. But it's a thoroughly miserable experience.

'You're doing well, Julian,' John says.

'Doesn't feel like it,' I say.

'Look, it's a long recovery.'

'No shit.'

I feel bad for John, it's not his fault that I've got to go through this, but it's not my fault either. I'm feeling really frustrated, and wish I hadn't bothered coming into this poxy place today.

I look around, trying to take my mind off the pain and frustration of this situation. This treatment room is not much to look at.

I can see John's stand-up skeleton, and some other fitness bits and pieces. This is so depressing. I just want to play football.

I don't want to be stuck in this Portakabin, while the lads are on the training pitch. If I'm not out there with them, the only other place I want to be right now is the pub. The place where I've been spending most of my time recently. Maybe too much time.

'One more stretch,' says John, interrupting my thoughts about sipping a cold beer.

'If I have to,' I say, resigning myself to my fate.

As John starts to push down on my leg and the knee starts to bend a little further, I clench my teeth, my buttocks, my fists and anything else I can squeeze together.

'For fuck's sake!' I shout, as a last resort, when I run out of things to clench.

'Fuck! Fuck! Fuck!' I follow up with. I'm not much of a conversationalist these days.

'Well done,' I hear John say. 'Let's go to the gym.'

I grunt. I can hardly hide my complete lack of enthusiasm for the gym, where more pain and boredom awaits me.

I shuffle off the treatment bed, and walk towards the door. If you can call this walking.

My knee is in a brace which helps me walk but I'm moving around like someone four times my age.

I 'walk' into the gym. This so-called gym could really do with a bit of love, I think, as I walk in there and survey the scene.

There are weights all down one side of the tiny room, and those brown wooden school benches down the other. Paint is peeling off the walls, and the room stinks. It should be condemned, knocked down and rebuilt. It's truly awful. A bit like me, considering how I'm feeling.

I know what's coming next. He's going to get the weights out, and he's going to make me do step-ups, with and without the weights. John sure knows how to have fun.

'Come on, Julian,' I say to myself. I know I just need to get *this done and then I can get out of here, another day chalked off, like I'm some kind of prisoner, barred from playing football until I've served my sentence.*

I certainly won't be let out early for good behaviour, I think, as I swear my way through the step-ups, not because they hurt that much, but more because of how I'm feeling in general.

The real pain is done, administered by John's healing hands. This is like death by boredom. Step up, step down, up, down, up, down. I'm telling you, this gym thing will never catch on.

But what choice do I have? I know this is what I need to do if I'm going to get back on that pitch with my team-mates.

That's the thought that I try to stay with as I complete another set of step-ups. John gives me a weight to hold to see how my knee copes with that.

I give it a go, and it's a breeze, so John gives me a heavier weight as if to say 'don't get clever, son, that was just for starters.'

This one's harder, and my leg and knee are starting to feel the strain, and I'm starting to feel annoyed because this is taking forever, and it's tough.

I put the weight down, and look at John. 'Fuck this, John. Fuck this. I can't do this anymore, I just want to play football.'

'I know this is not what you need to hear right now,' he says, which I'm thinking is not a great start, 'but, if you want

to get back to playing, this is the only way. There are no short cuts, it's bloody hard work, but you can do it.'

'I can't face doing this, week in, week out, forever,' I say. 'I just can't.'

I'm feeling awful now, absolutely shattered and low as anything. Nobody understands me, or what this is like for me. John looks at me sympathetically, but what else can the poor sod say or do when faced with a miserable, stubborn bastard like me?

'All I'm doing at the moment is coming in here, or going to the pub,' I tell him. 'I spend that much time in the pub that I'm worried I might be becoming an alcoholic. Without the football, there's nothing stopping me. I need to do something else, apart from just coming in here for an hour and doing these exercises, or I'm going to go mad.'

'Where did that come from?' I think to myself, and John must be thinking that too, given the look on his face. It's kind of a relief to say it out loud. I've been thinking it for long enough, but couldn't say it to anyone. But it's true, this is the situation, and it's not great.

'I hear you,' says John. 'Tell you what, let's finish up here for today, and I'm going to ring the surgeon to see what else he thinks you could do, to give you some more options.'

'Ok mate,' I say, 'Thanks.' John pats me on the shoulder, trying to encourage me. I do feel a bit better but still not great. The reality of the situation is bleak.

I leave the gym, and then go to the changing room to put the rest of my gear on. It's quiet in there, the lads are all still out on the pitches. It's weird to be in here on my own. It smells the same as always, looks the same as always, but it's not the same, because I should be out there with everyone else.

I walk out of there, away from that depressing place. I'm about to head out of the training ground, when I stop. I want to go and see the lads. I turn around and slowly make my way out to the pitches where they're training.

I decide not to go too close. I don't want to be a distraction. The boys are all working hard. I can hear a lot of banter and laughing, and why wouldn't they be having fun? Not only are they training and doing the thing they all love, but they're in the middle of a brilliant unbeaten run in the league, and are smashing it in the FA Cup too.

The atmosphere is really good, and I would give anything to be a part of it. I watch them do some drills, a few set-piece routines, and then a game.

I'm kicking every ball, jumping for every header and crunching into every tackle – all in my head of course. It's not much, but it's all I've got right now.

I can see that the session is winding down, so I walk back towards the Chadwell Heath entrance gates. I don't want to get in anyone's way when they're coming off the pitch. I'm not part of that scene at the moment, so I just feel like keeping my distance.

It's time to head back towards home. The pub is waiting for me – Rome wasn't built in a day.

•

It all started one October day in my home city. West Ham were playing against Bristol City at Ashton Gate where there was a dip on the side of the pitch, and as I went up for a header, I landed in this little dip, and fell off the pitch.

It felt a bit awkward but there was no pain at the time, although my left knee just did not feel right. It felt a bit limp and loose, but, as it wasn't painful, I carried on playing the rest of the game, as there were only around 10 minutes left, and I'm not the kind of player who doesn't finish a game unless there's a serious problem.

Rob Jenkins was still the physio at that point – you know, the bloke with the special bottle of medicine in his kit bag. He examined my knee after the game and felt that it was loose but thought that I might get away with it with a bit of luck. However, by the time I'd gone to see all my family in town that evening, it had started to swell up which was clearly not a good sign.

It wasn't looking good, but with no major pain and plenty of rest in between, Rob was hopeful I could play the next game against Swindon, which I did. But, only 38 minutes in, I went in for a tackle and my knee locked up, so I had to come off.

I was definitely very concerned now, but Rob still remained optimistic that we might get away without any surgery, and that staying off my feet in between games could help it. He said I could play the next game against Blackburn, but I wasn't sure at all. The gaffer was happy to go along with Rob's advice, so he named me in the starting line-up for the Rovers game, and it would be a very long time before he did that again.

This time, I lasted a fair bit longer, but around 10 minutes from the end, I jumped for a header, and my knee buckled when I landed. That was game over for me and my knee.

I went to see the club doctor, a bloke called Brian Roper who was old school and had been doing that job forever, although admittedly he did have medical qualifications. Unfortunately, he didn't see what John Green saw. John was the club's new, qualified, physio who was in the process of taking over from Rob Jenkins.

Roper thought I needed a simple cartilage operation from which I would recover so quickly that I could be back playing in six weeks. John, however, thought the state of my knee was consistent with ruptured cruciate ligaments, a different surgery and a far longer recovery.

Unfortunately for me, Roper was in charge of my case and he removed my cartilage. When I came round from the operation, he actually told me that he'd found tears on both my anterior and posterior ligaments but presumed they were from an old injury so left them.

It didn't sound good to me, but at that point I thought that as he was the surgeon, he knew exactly what he was doing so it wasn't for me to be asking questions. How wrong I was.

After the surgery, John Green spent little more than a month strengthening my quads and hamstring to support my knee, and I was back in a West Ham shirt for a reserve game against Reading. But within 15 minutes, both the shirt and myself were off, as my knee gave way again.

At this point, Billy Bonds and the coaching staff conceded that John's diagnosis looked right, but incredibly the gaffer still wanted me to go back to Roper so that he could re-assess the injury.

'Fuck that,' was my typically understated response. 'No way am I seeing him again.'

Billy was in a tricky position because Roper was on the club's payroll, but there was no way I was going back to see him, as he'd only succeeded in making my knee worse. I offered to pay out of my own pocket to see someone else privately to show Billy and the powers that be how desperate I was to get it sorted.

Eventually, John Green convinced the club to let me see a surgeon called John King at the London Independent Hospital in Mile End. He examined my knee, and his assessment was brutal and frightened the life out of me. 'We're not fucking messing around here, Julian. This is a nasty injury.'

I was immediately panicked by his tone. My worst fears were close to being realised when he told me that I may have only a one in ten chance of making a comeback and playing again. I felt so physically sick at hearing this, that I came very close to vomiting all over his consulting room floor.

I was only 22, and I just felt that there was no way this could be happening. At the time, I thought that if I heard that at 32, I would be gutted, but might understand it after a long playing career. But at this stage? No way, it just didn't make any sense and felt completely unfair.

What made me even angrier was the fact that I'd wasted two months since the original surgery. I could already have been two months closer to making a comeback if I'd have had the right operation back in October. And I was concerned that all those comebacks I'd tried to make in that time had actually damaged my knee even more.

Three weeks later, I went under the knife and John Green was present at the surgery – I'll never forget his post-op description of all the blood that came pouring out of my knee when they opened it up. It was horrific to think it had got into such a bad state since the original injury I had at Ashton Gate.

The fight to get back playing again started immediately after the operation. And I had to work so hard for everything because, back then, this was still a new type of football injury and the club didn't really know how to handle it.

For starters, I had to use an isokinetic machine in Harley Street. And if you don't know what that is, then don't worry, neither do I. I just knew that I had to use it as part of my recovery. I'd sit in the machine and it would move my leg, bend it, straighten it, and work all the muscles. At that stage, a machine like that was only available in Harley Street, so I was required to go there twice a week.

I was living out in Billericay at the time, so I called West Ham's taxi firm who drove all the way out there to pick me up, then took me to the Devonshire Hospital in central London. Once there, the cab waited outside for me for about an hour while I did my isokinetic thing, before driving me all the way back to Billericay. I think the cab fare came to about £260.

I was carrying on my rehab at the training ground the following day when Billy called me in to see him.

'What's this taxi bill?'

'It's for my rehab at the hospital,' I replied.

'You can't do that!'

'What?'

'You can't have a bill like that for a taxi twice a week,' he insisted.

'So how am I supposed to get there?'

'Jump on a tube.'

'Are you taking the piss? I'm on crutches and I've got a brace on my leg, how am I supposed to get on the tube?'

'Well, you definitely can't get a taxi.'

'Why don't you get me an automatic car from Dagenham Motors, and I'll drive up there?' I suggested, I thought quite reasonably.

'No, I can't do that. If I do that for you, I'll have to do that for everybody.'

'But I'm out for over a year, not everyone has this kind of injury.'

'No, I can't do that,' he said, while thinking. 'What I'll do is, I'll get Charlie the security guard to take you up there.'

'Charlie?' I replied.

'Yeah, Charlie.'

'Ok then.'

Charlie was a fantastic character. He was about 5 ft 6 and around 65 years old. He used to be on the gate, doing security at the training ground. Every time you'd drive in or out of Chadwell Heath, he'd give you a wave. You hadn't been to the training ground if you hadn't been waved in or out by Charlie.

When Harry was the manager we used to have these nine-a-side games on the five-a-side pitch, and the losing team had to pay £5 each which would go to some of the staff, so Charlie would always pick up £20. Everyone loved Charlie, he was one of those old boys who you could have a right old laugh with, and he was as much a part of West Ham as Moore, Hurst and Peters.

The only problem with Charlie was that he also happened to be one of the worst fucking drivers you've ever seen. That, and he was driving me to my hospital appointments in his claret and blue Ford Fiesta with West Ham down the side of it. It got to the point where I stopped caring whether I was going to recover from my injury, because I was just focusing on getting out of Charlie's car in one piece.

He was one of those drivers who had so many near misses on the road, that every time you got from A to B unscathed, it felt like you'd just been part of something miraculous. He got so close to the other cars, that he'd regularly clip wing mirrors, and think nothing of it.

But, because he was a bit of a legend around Chadwell Heath, I did appreciate his efforts and, on the way back from hospital, we'd always stop to pick up fish and chips or whatever he fancied. We'd then eat it together in the West Ham-branded Fiesta, before he'd drop me back at the training ground.

I honestly don't know how I survived those journeys with Charlie, but I do look back at them with a kind of fond terror if there's such a thing. A few years later, I went to Charlie's funeral as I wanted to pay my respects to a top bloke.

In the end, I was out for 14 months to the day. It was an incredibly long time to not be playing football. I know that if it wasn't for John Green and John King there is no way I would have made it back. The recovery was both intense and immense, but they helped me get through it.

After I confided my concerns to John Green about my state of mind and the fact that I was spending a lot of time in the pub, John King suggested I take up golf to help fill my days. His theory was that I was wearing a brace so I couldn't do any more damage to my knee.

'Fuck that, it's an old man's game,' was my immediate response, but that eventually gave way to my desperate need to relieve the boredom of this long, football-less lay-off. Suddenly, if anyone wanted to know where I was, it wasn't the pub, it was either the driving range or the golf course.

And it turned out that I was quite good at golf. I would go and practise every day, hitting loads of balls after training, and I'd always try to play at least nine holes a day.

It definitely helped, but there were still hard times. Sometimes, I'd wake up in the morning and I could not face going in for yet more tedious rehab work. John Green was really understanding, and he would say 'no problem, I'll see you tomorrow' but I couldn't push my luck and try that too often as he wouldn't let me get away with that.

If I tried that one too many times, he would tell me in no uncertain terms to get my arse into the training ground because otherwise I risked delaying my recovery. John was so good for me because he understood how I felt mentally, and I was happy to confide in him.

The problem with being out with a long-term injury is that it can often be a case of out of sight, out of mind. Not necessarily with my team-mates as they were great, Jimmy Quinn and Trevor Morley were there in hospital as soon as I'd had the operation, and everyone would ask me how

I was getting on, so that was good. Jimmy lived nearby in Billericay, and he was really good at keeping tabs on me throughout the long injury lay-off.

But it was more about the manager and coaches not really taking much interest in me. Sometimes, they would walk right past me as if I wasn't there. For them, I wasn't part of their plans for at least a year so it felt like they just forgot about me. As much as I understood that I wasn't their priority, I also needed to know that I was still part of the club.

As good as John Green was in terms of providing me with support, there were times when I needed to talk to Billy Bonds or one of the coaches, but they might have thought, 'Oh, he's Julian Dicks, he's strong, he doesn't need us' but deep down, I really did.

What I really wanted was for Billy to give me a bollocking for moping around and not getting my head down and getting on with my recovery. It's about knowing what your players need, and I found it tough that I felt so isolated.

There was one time when I arrived at the training ground and nobody was there, apart from John and some of the other injured lads. Nobody had mentioned to me that the players were having a golf day so there was no training that day. One day I was club captain, the leader of the pack, the next I was essentially a nobody. I was totally out of the loop.

The truth is that although I was determined to make a complete recovery, I didn't know if I would play again. That's what I had hanging over my head every hour of every day.

So, it hurt me that if I turned up at the ground on a match-day to support the lads, and was up in one of the lounges with the chairman and directors, none of them ever said a word to me. They just blanked me.

Someone had also spread rumours that my playing career was over, so I'd sometimes get commiserations from fans who I might meet out and about, and I had no idea what they were talking about. There were some sick people out there, spreading false information, but it only served to make me even more determined to get back playing again.

At that time, my twin girls were only two, so that really weighed heavily on my mind – how would I provide for them if I had to retire in my early twenties? It's not like today's game where if I'd played a few top-flight seasons, I'd already be a multi-millionaire. Far from it. So there was extra concern, and motivation, for me right there.

John Green was happy with my progress though, especially when I told him that when I'd crossed the road, I'd inadvertently broken out into a little jog and felt no adverse effects. From that point on, we stepped up the rehab and I was able to get on the treadmill. Slowly but surely, the light at the end of the tunnel was starting to glow brighter.

Soon enough, I removed the brace I'd been wearing on my leg for what felt like forever, which was another huge milestone. Suddenly, what had been the slowest, most boring and depressing process had become one that had gained some huge momentum.

I was getting carried away and was desperate to play again, especially once I'd returned to training with the lads. John wisely told me to hold off from playing for a few weeks, but they could only hold me back for so long. After more than a year without playing any meaningful football, I simply couldn't wait any longer.

Eventually, I was named in a West Ham reserve team to play against Ipswich at the Terence McMillan Stadium, a small football and athletics venue in Plaistow. I was chomping at the bit, and it wasn't just me that was raring to go.

The fans were also that excited about my comeback that some of them turned up at Upton Park to see the game – apparently, they'd been ringing the club to find out where the match was being played and someone had given the poor sods the wrong information. Luckily, a few fans did make it down to the right ground, and there was a huge cheer when I made my first tackle.

At one point, there was a 60:40 challenge in my opposite number's favour, and I just flew in there, won the ball and hit him hard in the process. I got straight back up, but it took the other man a while longer.

'Why the fuck did you do that?' he said while scrambling back to his feet.

'Well, I just had to try my knee out,' was my honest and accurate response.

Having come through that game without any problems, I was like a dog that had been let off the lead, and was desperate to play in the first team again. Unfortunately, my recovery had also seen me pile on the weight, and I was probably about a stone and a half heavier than I'd been when I first got crocked. Like I said, I'd spent a lot of time drinking, and the golf didn't exactly help me work up a sweat. Undeterred, I banged on the gaffer's door and told him that I was ready to play.

'No, you're not,' was his typically forthright response.

'Bill, I'm ready!' I said, practically begging him, while he looked at me with a face that suggested he didn't necessarily agree. 'If you need me, I'm ready,' I said.

Chris Hughton had joined from Spurs while I was recovering and, as luck would have it for me, not him, he got injured soon after my reserve team comeback. Suddenly, Billy almost had no choice but to recall me to the starting line-up and I was named in the side to face Sheffield United, exactly 14 months after I'd played my last game for the club.

From the point of view of my knee, the game went very well as I didn't have any problems. The fans were unbelievable, and supported me throughout the match, giving me an incredible reception when my name was announced.

The game was heading for a 0–0 draw when I misjudged a through-ball, and Brian Deane nipped in to score. I was gutted, but incredibly, I had an instant chance to make amends when we won a penalty soon after. In my absence,

Mike Small had been on spot-kicks, but he'd already been subbed, so I grabbed the ball, relishing the opportunity.

I'm not saying I hit that penalty hard, but I am saying there might have been about 14 months' worth of pent-up frustration that I channelled into striking that ball which flew into the net, to make it a far better comeback than it had been on course to be just a few minutes earlier.

There was a funny moment a few games later when we were playing Leeds United, and got another penalty. Mike Small picked up the ball and went to put it on the penalty spot. But there was no way on earth that I was going to let him take that penalty.

'What the fuck are you doing?' I asked him as he put the ball down.

'I'm taking the pen,' he replied.

'No, you're fucking not!' I said, replacing the ball on the spot.

Leeds striker Lee Chapman tried to put me off by telling me that I was going to put it over the bar, but I just ignored him, and smashed it into the net. Normal service had been resumed. We may have lost the game, but I still picked up the man of the match award and was just loving being back playing every week.

It was all I've ever wanted to do, and I had come so close to losing that. To retire at 22 would have been completely unthinkable, yet it so nearly happened. John Green and Billy Bonds both told me that other players may never have recovered from the injury I sustained. It meant I would always play football with a new appreciation that I had never previously had.

Fast forward a few years, and that troublesome knee started playing up again. There was a stage when I could manage it by playing, and not training while the swelling went down, then getting myself ready for the next game, and repeating the process.

I was 27, and it was far from ideal, but it was the best I could do. Eventually, surgery was the only option – I ended up having seven operations on that knee – and I faced another very lengthy lay-off, missing the entire 1997/98 season.

That period of rehab was very different to the first one though, as I had a much better idea of what to expect this time around as a result of my previous experiences and didn't get remotely close to becoming an alcoholic as I had done when I was 22.

But, even when I made my comeback from that second very long spell on the sidelines, it was never quite the same. I was 29 by then, and it just didn't feel fair that I was looking down the barrel of the end of my career.

There were other players whose careers lasted until well into their mid-30s and they didn't seem to give a shit about football. And someone like me, who put everything into every minute of every game for Birmingham, West Ham and

Liverpool, who lived to play football, then has their career cut short.

Although my last game for West Ham was a 4–0 home defeat by Arsenal in 1999, I think it was really all over for me when we played Charlton away a bit earlier in the season, and Harry Redknapp played me as a wing-back. It was a position I'd never previously played, and we lost 4–2.

•

I'm fuming. Nothing's even happened yet, but I'm angry. The gaffer's asked me to come and see him after training, and it's not going to be good news.

He's not exactly going to offer me a new contract, is he? Not after the absolute stinker I had on Saturday.

I'm in the shower, and I can't help but think about how this is going to go. My knee's aching. Maybe I shouldn't train tomorrow.

In a way, the knee is the least of my worries right now. I grab a towel and dry off.

I can hear the younger lads bantering. Reminds me of myself when I first came here. I look around the changing room, as I get dressed. So many unfamiliar faces now, but a load of new, decent lads all the same.

The team spirit is still strong – the faces change, but the place doesn't. Chadwell Heath is still a bit of a dump, with its old Portakabins and Romford charm.

I nod a goodbye to some of the boys as I walk out of the changing room, and head towards Harry's office.

I think about this being John Lyall's office, Lou Macari's, Billy Bonds' and now Harry's.

So many times I walked in here for a bollocking off Billy, and I'd end up rowing with him. It all feels very familiar.

I walk in and Harry's on the phone. Probably trying to sign my replacement, or something.

He beckons me over to sit down, which I do while he finishes his call.

I look around the office. I feel like I know it so well. The desk, the chair I'm sitting in. The piles of papers that seem to have been on that desk since I signed a contract for John Lyall.

Then there's the old stapler, the pens and some trays with more piles of papers in them.

I don't know what the average office desk looks like, given that I'm a footballer, but I'm guessing that this could be any office worker's desk.

Harry puts the phone down, and looks up at me.

'How's the knee?' he says, in his usual friendly tone.

'Not bad,' I reply. 'I might need to take tomorrow off, do that one day on, one day off, I've been doing.'

'I'm not too sure about that,' says Harry. 'I'd rather you were down here every day, with all the rest of the lads. I can't really have different rules for you.'

'But that's what I've been doing to manage it,' I say, as I feel myself starting to get wound up. Am I going mad, or

what? This was the bloke who was happy for me to train when I could until recently, so what's changed?

I don't have time to get that thought out, because Harry says, 'Look, we've got Newcastle at the weekend, and you're going to be on the bench.'

I don't have to think too hard about my reply.

'Not a fucking chance! There's no way I'm going to Newcastle and sitting on the bench. Pay me up and I'll leave.'

'Woah! Steady on, there's no way that's going to happen,' says Harry.

But my mind is made up. I just want to get out of this room as soon as possible. I can see how this is going. I've seen it before with other players.

Harry's talking to me, but the words aren't going in. I know what it's like once Harry doesn't want you.

He's the best manager in the world when he wants you. Encouraging you, putting his arm around your shoulder, giving you advice, loads of praise. Everything you need, basically.

But once he doesn't want you, it changes. And I'm sure that this is that moment. And with my knee in the state that it is, this is probably the end of my career.

Suddenly, he wants me to train every day even with my knee in the state it's in? Another clear sign of how the tide has turned. Typical Harry.

All of these thoughts come flooding into my mind. There's so much to take in, but I can't really take any of it in right now. I just need to get out of here.

'So that's how we're going to play this one from here, ok?' says Harry.

I haven't been listening to anything he's been saying. I need to clear my head and think about things properly.

'Ok,' I mumble, but only because I just need to get out of this room right now.

I walk out of there, and head straight for my car. I can see the pitches in the distance, the training fields where so much has happened over the years.

It's more than 10 years since I first walked through the gates that I'm about to drive out of. It won't be the last time, because I know that I need to be professional.

I know that I haven't played my last game for West Ham, but I also know that this feels like the beginning of the end.

That can't be right. It seems impossible. But if Harry doesn't want me, then I can't see any other clubs taking a chance on me with my crocked knee.

This thought is going over and over in my head, as I get into the car, start the engine, and drive towards the gates.

It ain't over til the fat lady sings, so they say. I try to tell myself this, as I go through the gates and start my journey home.

But as much as I try, in my heart, I know the truth. The fat lady isn't singing, but I think I can hear her clearing her throat and doing her warm-up exercises.

THE KOP

My left foot and a can of beans

I pick up my seven-iron and place my ball down carefully. I survey the scene ahead of me.

I can feel my heart beating ever so slightly quicker than usual, which is probably to be expected, considering what I'm about to do.

I look up and see my playing partner Neil Ruddock, or Razor as he's known to everyone, grinning at me so I smile back. Am I really about to do this? Too right, I am.

'Ready?' I say to Razor.

'Ready when you are,' he replies.

I place my feet on either side of the golf ball, and put a very small bend in my knees until I feel totally comfortable in my position.

I've taken tens of thousands of swings like this over the last few years, so it all feels completely natural to me, although I've not really hit a ball in this kind of environment previously.

I raise the seven-iron high behind my back and above my head, and I remember smashing golf balls through the open window of a hotel room with Frank McAvennie.

That was before I knew how to even hold a club. Very different times indeed.

I swing hard, make a sweet connection and the ball flies off through the air, over a field and into the players' car park at Melwood, Liverpool's training ground.

It looks like it bounces just short of a Porsche. Not mine, thankfully.

'Unlucky,' says Razor, chuckling to himself, while placing his ball down, and picking up a club.

I watch him stand over his ball, and then smash it high into the Merseyside sky, but it shoots off left, a mile wide of the car park.

'Useless!' I say, at the same time as picking up another ball, and setting myself up again.

This time, I make an even sweeter connection and I watch, half in horror, and half impressed with my ability, as the ball's arc takes it over the pitch immediately in front of us, and all the way on to John Barnes' Mercedes Benz SL.

'Woah!' says Razor, and immediately starts laughing. I'm laughing too. This is the most fun I've had at Melwood in months, and certainly beats training with the youth team, which is what I've been doing for weeks.

Now, Razor's lining up another ball and before I've even finished laughing, he launches it across Melwood, towards the players' car park again. We hear a noise, but can't see what he's hit.

We hit a few more with varying degrees of success, and I

feel happier than I have done in a long time. Razor's pissing himself laughing too.

I hear some shouting in the distance. We look at each other, and I shrug.

Then I hear a shout again, and it's louder and maybe a bit closer this time.

In no time at all, Razor and I pick up our clubs and balls, and run off, like a pair of schoolchildren who've been caught getting up to no good.

And that's what we are, I think, as I run back towards the main training ground, far away from the other side of the place where some scumbags have been hitting golf balls at expensive cars.

I'm not sure I even care if we do get rumbled. Things could hardly get any worse for me up here anyway. I'm so far from the first team, I might as well be an Anfield season ticket holder – except they get much closer to the starting line-up than I do.

And I know the likes of Barnes, Ian Rush and Steve Nicol will be completely unimpressed with our little game, but I don't give a fuck.

There are certain people at this club who dislike me anyway, so what difference does it make if I take a few pot-shots at their cars with my seven-iron? Are they going to dislike me even more? I doubt it.

So to hell with them, and the coaching staff and anyone else who doesn't rate me around here.

I've had enough of not playing football when I'm not even injured – that's the really annoying part. I missed so much football when I was physically incapable of playing, but when that's no longer the case, it pisses me off.

Anyway, what has any of that got to do with me hitting golf balls into a car park full of footballers' expensive cars? Everything and nothing I suppose. It was damn funny though.

•

So how on earth did I end up smashing golf balls in the Liverpool training ground?

I think the move to Liverpool probably came about as a result of a game I played for West Ham at Coventry. Which does sound a bit weird, admittedly.

It was early in the 1993/94 season, and the Hammers were struggling in our first season in the Premier League. Ok, we'd only played two games, but we'd lost them both and not scored a goal either. And we were heading up to the Midlands to take on a Coventry side who, believe it or not, were the early league leaders.

We went 1–0 up in the first half, and soon after I got into a tussle with Coventry's Micky Gynn. I was on the ball heading out of our penalty area, trying to clear any danger, but Gynn had his arms all over me, clearly fouling me. There was no referee's whistle, so I had to defend myself. I swung out an arm behind me and my elbow connected with him, and this time the ref did blow up.

Weirdly, I was booked but we were awarded the free-kick, but I think that was because Gynn made the most of the situation that he'd instigated, and conned the ref. It was the kind of thing that happened on the pitch the whole time, and I can't say I thought anything of it, until we got back to the dressing room at half-time.

I'd barely walked through the door when Billy Bonds said, 'You fucking wanker!'

I was stunned, and immediately looked behind me, assuming he must have been talking to someone else. But he was staring straight at me.

'Me?' I asked him, pointing to myself.

'Yeah, fucking elbowing someone and nearly getting sent off. You could have cost us the fucking game,' he yelled at me. He was fuming, and now, so was I. Who the fuck was he to have a go at me about elbowing players?

'That's a bit pot calling the kettle black coming from you,' I replied. 'You used to elbow everybody!'

'I should take you off,' he said to me. Take me off? Take me off? I was incensed, and I ripped my shirt off, and threw it right at him, before adding 'fuck you!' for good measure.

There was no way I was putting up with the way he was talking to me – I've never let anyone talk to me like that if I felt it wasn't justified, and this was no exception.

Suddenly, the two of us were squaring up right there in the dressing room, and we had to be pulled apart by Harry Redknapp and some of the players.

I walked off into the showers and as I stormed off, he yelled, 'See me in the gym on Monday morning!' which meant he wanted us to sort it out like men at the training ground.

In the heat of the moment, that kind of thing got said fairly often, but that's all it was. It was just words as passions were running high. So many things like that were said in changing rooms and if you took it personally, you'd fight everyone.

Harry came into the showers to tell me I had to go out for the second half, and soon I was back in my discarded shirt and out on the pitch, ready to do it all again.

On the Monday morning, Billy did call me into his office for a word, but not into the gym for a showdown. To be fair to him, he apologised for his part in the bust-up, and we shook hands and moved on. But I couldn't resist a final jibe.

As I stood by his door to leave the room, I said, 'Bill, I would have ripped your fucking head off!' and quickly closed the door behind me.

But maybe I didn't get the last laugh, because, as I said, that whole Coventry incident may well have led to me leaving West Ham for Liverpool. With all the red cards the season before, I knew that Harry wasn't necessarily my biggest fan back then, and it was him who orchestrated the move to Anfield.

It wasn't just about getting me out the door because maybe they didn't think I was worth the trouble. It was also about my value, and where they might be able to improve a squad that was clearly going to struggle at that level, as subsequent results showed.

Harry set up a deal where the club were able to get David Burrows and Mike Marsh in from Liverpool to replace me, while they also signed Lee Chapman up front as well. Not a bad piece of business, but it did mean the end of my first spell at West Ham.

I didn't really want to leave, but it didn't feel like I had much of a choice. When Harry suggested I go and speak to Liverpool manager Graeme Souness because the deal was done, what else could I do? Once I met up with Graeme and realised we were cut from the same cloth when it came to our black and white attitude to the game, I wanted to sign for him.

And I'd be lying if I said that the opportunity to join one of the biggest clubs in the world wasn't attractive. Who wouldn't want to play at Anfield, in front of the Kop, a place of such incredible football history?

When I first signed for Liverpool, I was staying at the Haydock Thistle hotel, right next to the racecourse, because I hadn't sorted out a house yet. On my first weekend, the All Blacks were also staying in the hotel. I was tucking into my breakfast on Saturday morning, when they all came down from their rooms.

And what a sight that was. Huge man mountains moving through the hotel, and each of them carrying a crate of beer. Except all the cans in each crate were empty. They'd obviously had a massive night, as I'd done once or twice in a hotel room, and were then tidying up after themselves. I remember being impressed that I might have been on the same wavelength as these giant physical specimens, and it gave me a lift as I prepared to start life at my new club.

Ahead of my Liverpool debut, I turned up at Melwood in a chauffeur-driven limo organised by the club, but I was soon brought back down to earth when Bruce Grobbelaar chucked all of his dirty kit at me when I joined my new team-mates in the changing room. To be honest, that made me feel quite welcome.

Bruce was a fucking loon. Genuinely one of a kind. He'd tell me about him fighting during the war in Zimbabwe, while he was never shy to share his stories about wrestling crocodiles. He was obviously a character on the pitch too, taking the ball out of the box to where the right-back would usually be, as if it was the most normal thing in the world.

I quickly found out just how off the wall Bruce was, as he was part of an infamous moment in my first game for Liverpool which was the Merseyside derby against Everton.

It didn't go well. I made a mistake which led to Tony Cottee making it 2–0 to Everton, after my old sparring partner Mark Ward had scored the first for them. That opening goal came from a corner that Steve McManaman only half-cleared to the edge of the box where Wardy was waiting to smash it in through the crowd of players. And Bruce went absolutely bonkers with Steve.

Things like that will often happen in training, as there's always going to be tension between players. But this was right in the middle of the Merseyside derby. The pair exchanged words, and suddenly they were slapping each other on the edge of the penalty area! I think my first thought was 'fucking hell', but I also found it quite funny. Here was Bruce, a bit of a character to say the least, losing the plot with Steve, who was a young lad at the time. It was absolute madness.

As far as debuts go, it was something of a baptism of fire, but despite my mistake Souness didn't have a pop at me. He'd actually been talking me up to the press, telling them that I had a 'left foot that could open a can of beans'. I'm not sure I was capable of that kind of trick, but I settled in at Anfield, and hit it off with a few of the players.

First up, there was Razor. I got on really well with him. He was very loud and very big, the kind of person you definitely wanted on your side if it all kicked off. He loved a drink, and was a good person to have in the dressing room for taking the piss, having a laugh and doing stupid things. As easily as he'd say hello to someone, Razor would cut your clothes up, cut your trainers in half, and stick Deep Heat in your pants. It was a part of the dressing room culture back then, that I can't imagine ever happening now. There was always something going to happen in the training ground with people like Razor around, which made the whole experience a lot more fun.

It soon became obvious that there were two distinct camps there, with the older lads like Ian Rush and Steve Nicol, and some of the younger ones like Robbie Fowler, Don Hutchison, Jamie Redknapp and Rob Jones. It was the younger lot who I felt I had more in common with. They were far more up for having a laugh, and going out for a drink, in the same way as I'd been used to doing at West Ham.

I also got on well with John Barnes, who was a lovely bloke, as well as Bruce, of course. I didn't get on that well with Rushy. I'm not sure he rated me that much, which was the case with some of the fans as well.

To be fair, my recurrent knee injury certainly didn't do me any favours in being able to perform at my best. I'd not been at Anfield that long when Oldham's Gunnar Halle smashed into my knee, which put me out of action for two months, as I had to have surgery to trim the cartilage.

I was obviously in the hands of the Liverpool doctors, but John Green was keeping tabs on my situation which was great as he knew the full history. It was a frustrating time, but after such a long lay-off previously, a couple of months was a drop in the ocean for me.

One of the strange things about my Liverpool spell was the lack of yellow cards being waved in my direction, and there was certainly no sign of a red. Because of the injury, I ended up playing just 28 games for the Reds, yet I only picked up one booking that entire time. And I honestly don't think I played the game any differently just because I was in a Liverpool shirt. I was as committed and aggressive as I would be in any game, and it made me suspect that a certain amount of protection came my way because I was a Liverpool player.

I've said it before, but I think my reputation as a hard man or a dirty player was as much because I was playing for West Ham, as it was because of anything I did on the pitch. I can't think of any other reason to explain my ridiculously low yellow card count at Liverpool.

Another thing that was lower at Liverpool was my goal count as Jan Molby was on penalties there – they obviously hadn't seen me take one before. I did get to take one when Jan was injured, and it turned out to be an extremely significant goal. We were playing Ipswich in April 1994, and Don Hutchison was brought down in the box, so I stepped up.

I hammered it low and hard to the keeper's left, then went to salute the Kop with my arms aloft. A great moment, by any standards. But it turned out to be an even greater moment when I discovered at the end of the season, that it was the last goal ever scored in front of the old standing Kop before the entire stand was rebuilt, and seats were put in. When you think about what that old Kop had witnessed, all those goals, and the goalscorers who stood in front of it celebrating with the fans, it's something that I'm still proud of to this very day.

Due to my injury earlier that season, I had missed playing against West Ham at Anfield, but I was very much part of the Liverpool team that went down to Upton Park later in the campaign.

Prior to that, to celebrate the opening of West Ham's new Bobby Moore Stand, I had been invited to play at Upton Park in a Bobby Moore Memorial match, so the Premier League game wasn't my first time back there. I got a great reception from the fans the first time, but when I went back there with Liverpool, it was absolutely amazing.

I knew I had a great relationship with the West Ham supporters, but they blew me away with the welcome they gave me, even though I was wearing a Liverpool shirt. I think they understood that if Liverpool come in for you, you're going to go. It wasn't a case of Paul Ince putting on a Man United shirt before he left for Old Trafford. I went to Liverpool because I had to, and the supporters got that.

I felt so at home playing back at Upton Park that at half-time, I walked down the tunnel, straight past the away team dressing room door, and was heading for the home team's changing room until the youth team manager Tony Carr stopped me with a smile on his face, and asked me where I was going! It was a funny moment, but one that also reminded me just how much West Ham was a part of who I was. It always felt like home.

Everything changed for me at Liverpool when Graeme Souness was replaced as manager by Roy Evans midway through the 1993/94 season. I'd signed to play for Souness, not for Roy, but I was used to changes like that after my West Ham experience when Lou Macari took over from John Lyall.

I was still happy enough at Liverpool as we'd found a lovely place to live, and the girls were very happy at school up there, so we were really settled. And the relationship with Roy wasn't bad at all – we even bumped into him at the airport when we were going on our summer holiday, and he told me to enjoy my break and not to worry about tabloid speculation that he wanted me to leave.

But it all started to go wrong when pre-season started, and we were hammered 4–1 by Bolton. In the changing room afterwards, Roy was livid, saying we'd embarrassed the club, and he singled out my fellow defender Mark Wright for criticism.

We were due to fly off to Germany a few days later for a pre-season tour, and when I asked one of the coaches Ronnie Moran if I needed to give my passport to the club, I was stunned when he said I didn't need to as I wouldn't be going on the trip. It was the first I'd heard of it.

Both myself and Mark Wright were left behind, with my brief to work on my fitness as Roy thought I was unfit and overweight. And there was me thinking that pre-season was the time to build fitness for the campaign ahead. To make matters worse, he told this to the press before he told me, which really pissed me off.

When I confronted him about it, he acknowledged that he shouldn't have done that, but I had my revenge soon after when some reporters came to the training ground while the rest of the squad were in Germany. They were looking for a story so I gave them one when I told them that Roy didn't have the bottle to tell me to my face that I wasn't going to Germany.

And that was pretty much it as far as my time with Liverpool went – I never played another game for the club, as Roy decided I wasn't for him. It was clear we didn't like each other.

What's more, I didn't get on with any of the coaches. Ronnie Moran and Steve Heighway were old school Liverpool, and always had a go at me for taking a ball out before training, because that's not how Bill Shankly used to do it, Even under Souness, the coaches would often berate me for having my Cokes and Mars bars in the dressing room before a game. They tried to explain to me that it wasn't good for my body to go out and play after that. But they failed to understand that's what I'd always done and it had never affected my performance in any way.

The only coach I had a decent relationship with was Sammy Lee, who was the reserve team manager. We got on well, but there wasn't much he could do when Roy banished me to train with the kids.

There were days when I'd turn up to training, stay in my car, then go back home as I just couldn't face the prospect of training with the youth team. It was a tough time, but that didn't stop me from having a good time away from Melwood.

Don Hutchison and I lived near each other and we spent a lot of time together, especially at our local pub. Given what I was going through at Liverpool, it was really important for me to be able to let my hair down, and Don was more than happy to be my partner in crime. He was having his own difficulties at the club, so we were both facing similar problems, which we addressed by getting drunk – perhaps not the best approach, but we had a lot of fun anyway.

There was one night when we were out together, the evening before a reserve team friendly against Altrincham. We started off in our local and ended up staying there until about 3 a.m., both very much the worse for wear. Don could barely make it out of the pub, so I helped him over to my house, where he slept in one of my girls' beds as they were staying out that night.

We had to meet at Anfield at 12 p.m., so I woke Don at 11.15 a.m. to find that he'd thrown up all over my daughter's bed. I dragged him to Anfield, and we got there just in time. We got on the coach, but he headed straight for the toilet at the back, and threw up again. He was that loud that I could actually hear him, but fortunately Sammy Lee didn't notice.

Eventually, the whole thing got me down. I went to see Roy Evans and told him that I wasn't willing to train with the kids anymore as I didn't think it was doing me any good, and

I strongly suggested that he might want to move me on if I wasn't going to be part of his plans.

It was around that time that I played in a reserve game against Everton and Tony Cottee was playing for them that day. We had a chat and he told me he was going back to Upton Park. The lucky bastard!

I was desperate to get out of Anfield and made no secret about it. I don't know if Harry Redknapp was keeping tabs on my situation through Jamie, but my prayers were answered when Jamie told me that his dad might be interested in taking me back to West Ham, as Harry was now in the hot seat on his own, with Billy Bonds having left the club. I told Jamie to tell his dad that I would have walked back down to the East End.

Even though I was owed money by Liverpool on my contract, it wasn't about the finances for me. It was far more about playing football, as I just wanted to be at a club where I was going to play, so I spoke to Harry and told him exactly that.

In the end, the Hammers did incredibly well on the deal to bring me back home, as they made a very decent profit on the transfer fee they received for me. I think Liverpool were probably happy to offload me, and I was absolutely delighted to get back to Upton Park in October 1994. Everyone was a winner.

And Don Hutchison also made the journey south, meaning we could carry on where we'd left off in Liverpool. One of my first games for West Ham after I returned was against Leicester on a Saturday, and I remember myself, Kenny Brown and Don went out on the piss in Romford on the Thursday night before, which was definitely not within the rules.

But rules are made to be broken, and it was just so good to be back.

•

I crack open a can of Coke, and take a few gulps. It's so good to be back. Back in my pre-match bath. Back at Upton Park. Back home.

The lads are on the pitch, warming up, and I'm in here doing my own warm-up, and nobody's breathing down my neck.

In many ways, I can't quite believe my luck. I've not played a Premier League game for what seems like years, yet that's about to change in less than half an hour. My Liverpool nightmare is finally over.

I drain the Coke, and get out of the bath, and back into the changing room. I look at all the shirts hanging out on the pegs, with names and numbers visible. It still seems strange to me that we have our names on our shirts, rather than just a number, but that's the way things are these days.

The last time I was in a first-team dressing room, the names on the shirts read Barnes, Rush, Fowler, Redknapp, McManaman, Nicol, Whelan, Jones. Now, as I look around the room I see Bishop, Miklosko, Allen, Potts, Cottee, Martin, Breacker. With all due respect to my former Liverpool team-mates, it's so good to be back.

I stop in front of the peg that says 'Dicks 3' and I pick up the shirt and pull it on over my head. What a feeling this is. The shirt hangs down over the top of my shorts. It's quite baggy, yet still sits quite snug on my belly, which is probably not the best news for me so close to kick-off.

I know I'm probably a few pounds too heavy at the moment, but I've not been playing or training properly for months so it's no surprise. And I've also spent a lot of that time in the pub, which hasn't done me any favours either.

There's no use crying over spilt milk. Or beer. I'm playing for West Ham in the Premier League against Southampton so I need to focus on the job in hand.

I pull my socks on, then my boots. As I do this, the dressing room fills up with all my team-mates. Slowly, every shirt with name and number on the back goes on to the bodies of every player.

I'm sitting quietly, looking around the room. I'm trying to soak it all up, take it all in. This moment. This really lovely moment.

I put my hand on my head, something I've been doing a lot in the last few days. I enjoy the feeling of my stubbly scalp, and I run my hand across it.

I've never had my head shaved this close before, but I

wanted to mark my return to Upton Park in some way. It's a fresh start, with a fresh, no-nonsense look.

I could probably do with shaving off a few pounds as well, but hopefully that'll happen as I get back to playing and training properly.

I'm pondering all of this as Harry comes into the dressing room. I sit down as Harry starts to speak about the game. He's reminding us what we need to do out there, but I'm not sure I need a team talk. If I'm not up for it today, when will I ever be up for it?

And I've never really needed to be told how to play. I think if I needed that, I shouldn't be a pro footballer.

I listen to Harry, anyway. He doesn't speak for long, then Alvin Martin yells a few words, with Lee Chapman chipping in too.

I stand up, and head for the door, along with everyone else – it's time.

I walk down the tunnel and, as the first players make their way through it and out on the pitch, I hear the roar of the crowd, a very familiar noise, but especially welcome today.

I emerge from the tunnel on to the pitch myself, and the noise increases enormously. I look around and everyone's on their feet, applauding. There are banners in the crowd saying 'Welcome Home' and I'm just amazed by this incredible reception.

Somewhere in the Bobby Moore Stand, my mum is watching on, joining in with the cheers no doubt. I raise my hands above my head and try to applaud the fans. It's the least I can do for these wonderful people who've always stood by me, no matter what.

I break out into a little jog, and continue to applaud the fans on the other side, as I head across the pitch. My pitch. The place where I really feel like I belong. What a feeling this is, and we haven't even kicked off yet.

It all feels like it's a bit of a blur as I start to do a few little warm-up stretches, and head to the left-back position, waiting to see which end we're kicking towards.

I'm very much in my own head right now, thinking about making that first challenge, getting that tackle in, getting that first touch of the ball.

What a surreal feeling this is, to be back here. So strange, but yet so familiar. It all seems to be happening so fast as we kick off, and there's no time to think anymore. I'm just playing.

I get on the ball. I win a tackle. I take a throw. It's all so normal. Except I haven't played Premier League football for a long time. I bomb forward a few times, and notice that it takes a little bit more out of me than usual.

But that doesn't matter, because here I am, doing what I love again.

Martin Allen has the ball and he smacks it against the crossbar. Should be 1–0. We need to win today, on my return.

Half-time comes and goes, and then it happens. Rush, Matthew not Ian, down the right, plays in Allen, and this time he smashes it into the net.

I'm fired up now, this is going to be our day. My day. The perfect day.

Southampton have the ball midway in our half on their right, and our left. My side. Nobody gets time on the ball over here.

I start running, and I'm almost at a full sprint now as one Saint plays it back to another, Paul Allen. My old friend.

I'm going full pelt, and I launch myself two-footed at Paul, going straight through him, but not quite making full contact. He kind of rides the challenge, but then goes down. Fair play to him, he's not made a meal out of it at all.

The referee Joe Worrall walks towards me, reaches into his shirt pocket, and shows me a yellow card.

I've got a straight face on, but I'm laughing inside.

One yellow card in 28 games for Liverpool! I've only been on the pitch for about an hour, and here's my first booking of my second spell at West Ham.

I walk back towards our penalty area, and get ready to defend the free-kick I've conceded.

What a feeling this is. God, it's good to be back.

PART TWO

THE GAFFERS

£650 a week? I'm going to be rich!

I'm walking off the training pitch, sweating heavily as I've given it everything I had. Obviously.

I can see the gaffer Garry Pendrey walking towards me, with a kind of purposefulness about him. I hope I'm not in any trouble – why is that always my first thought?

He's locked eye contact with me, so he obviously wants a chat. I look back at him and he says, 'Have a shower then come and see me.'

'Ok, gaffer,' I say, and I try to say it as confidently as possible although I've got no idea what he wants.

I'm intrigued, so I jog straight to the changing room to get showered and dressed as quickly as possible.

'What could this mean?' is almost the only thought I have as I throw my clothes back on after my speedy wash.

I'm pretty sure I haven't done anything wrong, so maybe it's good news? Although I don't know what that might be. Maybe I'm getting dropped? But that wouldn't make sense as I'm playing well, and have been all season.

'Something's definitely up,' I think as I tie my laces, and head out of the changing room, while most of my team-mates are still in the shower.

I walk down to Garry's office and knock on the door, then open it almost straightaway as he calls me in.

He's sitting at his desk, so I sit down in the chair opposite him. 'For fuck's sake, just say something,' I think, as I sit there.

'You'll have to come to the ground tomorrow because we've accepted a bid for you from West Ham,' he says.

'Fucking hell!' I think.

'Ok, no problem,' I say.

Garry continues to talk, but I can't hear what he's saying. West Ham! A First Division club! Me!

'Yeah, ok,' I hear myself saying, but I've got no idea what I'm saying that about. I've only ever been a Birmingham City player, but that looks like it's about to change. It's so much to take in, meaning it's hard to know what to even think or say.

Before I know it, I find myself out of his office and heading to my car. Tomorrow, I'll go to St Andrew's, Birmingham's home ground, and my life could change forever.

•

As I walk into one of the offices at St Andrew's, I'm not sure what I'm thinking. I know that West Ham want me, and I know that I'd love to go there. But, apart from that, I don't know how this meeting will go.

Some of my team-mates have agents, but I don't. I'm 19 years old, I'm still a teenager, still working out this game.

I open the door and immediately breathe in a lungful of smoke. It's coming from the cigarette which West Ham manager John Lyall is holding between his fingers, and it's certainly not the first one he's had while he's been in here.

I shake his hand, and then shake the hand of the man sitting next to him, who he tells me is Eddie Baily, the club's chief scout.

I'm ushered into a seat and then John starts talking, in between taking drags on his fag.

'We've had some good reports about you from Steve Whitton,' says John in a broad Cockney accent.

Steve is my team-mate at Birmingham, but he used to play for West Ham and is clearly still in touch with his former employers. That's nice of him.

'We need a left-back,' says John. 'And you're our choice.'

I'm not sure if I'm being asked or told what's happening here, but I like the way he's talking about me.

John crushes the butt of his cigarette into an ashtray, pulls another one out of his packet which is on the table in front of him, lights it up, and then says, 'Here's your terms. We'll give you £650 a week, a £50 appearance fee, and bonuses based on where we are in the league.'

'Fuck me!' I think. 'I'm going to be rich!' I don't know what to say. I'm being paid £140 a week to play for Birmingham, so this is another level altogether.

I realise I haven't said anything in reply to John. I'm trying to take it all in, while he takes in as much of his cigarette as he can.

This doesn't feel like it's a negotiation, but it also doesn't feel like there's much to argue about. But I need to let the missus know before I sign on the dotted line.

John takes another sharp drag of his fag, and I tell him that I need to call the wife.

I leave the room, and the haze of smoke from John's cigarettes, for a minute and head into another office to make the call.

As I dial our home number, I keep thinking about playing in the First Division for West Ham. And the £650 a week.

I wait for the ringing tones, but the bloody number's engaged. She's on the phone. I've got this offer and she's on a call.

'What should I do?' I think to myself. But I quickly realise that there's not much to think about here. Yes, it's a move away from the Midlands, but who's going to turn this down? I'm certainly not.

I march back into the room where John has just put out another fag, and he looks up.

'I'd love to sign for West Ham!' I tell him.

'I knew you would,' he says, smiling, offering me his hand which I suddenly find myself shaking. At the same time, all I can think is 'I'm going to play for West Ham'.

Yesterday, I was a Birmingham player, training with all the Birmingham players, all these team-mates who have been like older brothers to me over the last four or five years.

But, now I'm suddenly going to be a West Ham player. I can't stop thinking about this as I sit down opposite John *again, and he lights another cigarette. I mean we all like a smoke, but this bloke is something else.*

'What do you know about West Ham?' he says to me, blowing out a long breath of smoke at the same time.

It's a great question, and immediately I'm filled with panic. My mind goes straight to playing there with Birmingham, and how terrifying it was playing down the side of the infamous Chicken Run. I wasn't exactly made to feel welcome.

'Well, I know you, of course, Billy Bonds, and I know about the Chicken Run,' I say.

'Well, that's all you need to know,' says John.

'That's it?' I think, and then I hear myself saying: 'But John, the Chicken Run was brutal and horrible!'

'Trust me, son,' he says. 'They'll love you.'

I instantly believe him. Maybe it's the way he says it, but it makes me feel like this is going to go well. The bloke's been managing the Hammers for years. If anyone's going to know whether the fans will take to me, it's him.

We talk more, John smokes more, and I listen more. Everything's happening quickly. We agree that I'll come down to the training ground tomorrow to sign a contract.

My entire life is about to change.

•

The first time that my life changed so dramatically was when I was 14. That was when I left my family back in Bristol and headed to Birmingham to start what would become my football journey.

Aston Villa had a scout called Ron Veal, who was also very good mates with their manager Ron Saunders. He first saw me play when I was around 11 or 12. At that stage, I played for my school team, and also turned out for West Town Harriers, who were like the unofficial youth team of Bristol City.

Ron asked my dad if I'd like to come for trials at Villa, but my old man felt that I was a bit young at the time, and suggested that the scout came back when I was 14.

My dad knew what he was talking about. He'd had a decent career as an amateur player and went on to manage Shepton Mallet. I felt like he knew what was best for me.

Having said that, other clubs did take a look at me over the next couple of years, but I was a tiny little lad at that age, and Luton, Man City and West Ham all thought I wasn't big or quick enough to make it when I went to those clubs for trials.

But Ron Veal kept watching me and, like clockwork, as I approached my 14th birthday, he invited me for another trial with Villa. Well, he asked my dad, who then asked me, and I was obviously keen.

We all went over to Bodymoor Heath as a family and I remember how impressed I was with the facilities there. The training ground was exceptional, like nothing I'd ever seen before in terms of its size and everything it housed. It felt like we were in a resort hotel, or at least that's how it seemed to me back then.

After two days of training at Villa, Ron Saunders spoke with my dad and offered me the opportunity to sign schoolboy forms. That would mean me moving to live in Birmingham, going to school there, and training with Villa after school. At the age of 14, that was a massive change in my life.

At the time, I had been training with Bristol City and my dad spoke to the manager there to find out what his plans were for me. Alan Dicks – no relation – told my dad that I might break into the first team by the age of 23, and that was swiftly the end of my involvement with the Robins.

After speaking to Ron Saunders, my dad – as he always did – asked me what I wanted to do, and I decided this was too good an opportunity to turn down, even if it did mean upping sticks and leaving my family.

But within a week of making that decision, Ron Saunders had left his position at Villa and went to join their city rivals Birmingham, which could have thrown everything up in the air.

However, he called my dad to explain the situation and offered me the chance to join him at St Andrew's instead. When my dad told me and asked me what I wanted to do, I had no hesitation as I wanted to sign for Ron, not necessarily Villa or Birmingham. And that would be the same story throughout my career as I always signed for a manager rather than a club – it was true with John Lyall at West Ham and Graeme Souness at Liverpool.

And so at the age of 14, I left home. Bristol to Birmingham may have been less than 100 miles, but for me it was like moving to a different world, and I found it really hard. Suddenly, I was at a new school. I hated school at the best of times, but now I was at a new place, with new teachers and kids, and everyone knew why I was there.

Birmingham were happy for me to play for my new school team, and on the weekends I'd return home to Bristol to see my family. Although that had the effect of giving me some major Sunday night blues as I never wanted to go back to Birmingham. Those were hard times, as it meant I was effectively leaving my family again every week. As much as I didn't want to do that, I knew that in order to further my career, I had to make those sacrifices.

Don't get me wrong, I would not change any of it for one second. But those early years were tough. I was living in digs, boarding in someone else's home, going to a school I didn't know, removed from everything I'd known. It's not an easy thing to get through but thank goodness I stuck at it, or I would never have gone on to have the career I did.

And there were no guarantees either. Even though I'd signed forms which meant I would eventually get an apprenticeship and then turn professional, that still didn't mean I was going to make it. Of the boys who were with me at Birmingham, Ian Taylor and I were the only players who went on to have decent careers. There's so much hard work to do throughout those teenage years and beyond, and the fact that only a couple of us made it, tells its own story.

I was way more fortunate than most, as I was still an apprentice when I made my first-team debut. I'd been training with the first team for a while which meant I'd been shown no mercy on the training pitch, with none offered back. That was how it was. One Friday, I'd been cleaning my team-mates' boots, but come the Saturday I was their equal, sharing a pitch with them, despite only being 17 years old.

My debut was as a substitute in an away game at Chelsea but, never one to do things by halves, my first start was the derby against hated rivals Aston Villa at St Andrew's. Those were the days when I was an inside-left, and I wore the number 10 shirt.

I was aware of the enormous crowd watching, by far the biggest I'd ever played in front of, but the game seemed to pass by so quickly. It was a goalless draw, in which I very nearly scored the winner but Villa keeper Nigel Spink managed to save a fierce volley that I'd connected with really well. And that was it. In the blink of an eye, I'd played an entire professional football match.

With Ron Saunders as manager, and some of those no-nonsense pros like Pat Van den Hauwe, Noel Blake and Mick Harford at the club, there was no way I was going to be allowed to let my debut go to my head.

The following week, it was the same, in that we were still

steaming into each other during five-a-side in training, I was still cleaning boots, and I was definitely still living in digs and eating steak and drinking Guinness. My feet couldn't have been more firmly planted on the ground if I'd been standing in cement.

But things can change very quickly in football. One minute Ron Saunders was the manager, and the next he was gone. We lost to non-league Altrincham in the FA Cup, and he resigned, which may sound weird, but is something that managers used to do.

John Bond replaced Ron and called a team meeting. We were playing Man City at Maine Road, and he needed someone to put their hand up to play left-back, as our thin squad of 16 was stretched to the limit.

I was still an inside-left at that time, but something inside me made me raise my hand while thinking 'fuck it, why not?'

It must have gone reasonably well in Manchester, as I played at left-back again soon after when we faced Luton. I had a very good game, some might say a blinder, and it was after that match that I was asked to sign pro forms.

The fantastic Birmingham fans were always creating an unbelievable atmosphere. They were fucking nuts, to be honest. Those were the days of proper hooliganism and the Blues fans were known as the Zulu Warriors. So when I was playing in front of 35,000, and most of them were chanting 'Zulus' it made the hairs on the back of my neck stand up.

I think I got on ok with the fans. I remember getting hammered 6–0 by a Crystal Palace team that had Mark Bright and Ian Wright up front. Despite the score, I continued to give it everything I had, demanding the ball off the keeper so that we could build attacks, and I still went to clap the fans at the end, with no fear of getting any negativity from them because they knew I'd given 100 per cent.

Another thing I loved about Birmingham was that they allowed fans into the training ground to watch us train. I thought that was fantastic as it helped them connect with us and vice versa. I loved Birmingham, it was such a good club for me. There is no way I would have gone on to enjoy the career I had if I'd started elsewhere. Like I say, when you've got Mark Dennis smashing into you in training on a daily basis, you learn pretty fast. But it wasn't just about that. It was the sense of team spirit that stood me in such good stead. It was something that I took with me throughout my career.

My professional career at Birmingham didn't last long – it was just under three years before West Ham and John Lyall came calling – but I had an incredible experience there. All those years of steak and Guinness may well have taken their toll, but at least I wasn't that rake-like 14-year-old anymore, who was told he was too small to make it as a footballer.

So when I turned up at West Ham's Chadwell Heath training ground for the first time and I was greeted by my new team-mate Tony Gale suggesting that I looked a bit overweight, I was happy to laugh it off as banter – and there would be plenty more of that over the next 11 years.

•

The start of my first spell at West Ham was all about John Lyall. My old manager at Birmingham, John Bond, was a similar character, and he'd played more than 400 games for the Hammers. But John Lyall was out there on his own. He was a total gentleman, who couldn't do enough for you.

When I first signed for West Ham, I didn't have a car or a place to live so I was staying in a hotel in Epping. John would go out of his way to pick me up from the hotel, to take me to the training ground. And he would also drop me back at the hotel after training.

The only downside to that arrangement was his prolific chain-smoking. He would puff away for the duration of every journey, and the windows would always be up. It got to the point where I literally couldn't see out of the window as there was so much smoke in the car – god only knows how he could see where he was going. And because I was only 19, I was far too scared to ask him to open the windows.

Apart from the smoking, John was around 20 years ahead of his time. Our training sessions were great and he was very strong tactically. And his man management was second to none. I don't know anyone who disliked him, and he would still give you a bollocking if you needed it.

My feelings about John only got stronger when I attended a memorial dinner for him at Upton Park, soon after he sadly passed away in 2006. You only had to look around at all the great football men who turned up to pay tribute to this giant of the game, and they included Alex Ferguson. I didn't know it, but Fergie and John had been good friends for many years and Fergie had come down to the memorial in London purely to speak about their friendship, and how often they spoke to each other over the years. I'd never heard Sir Alex speak with such emotion and honesty, and that really changed my opinion of him, as I warmed to him after that night.

Mind you, his tongue was still as sharp as ever. When I was going up the stairs with my notoriously hard-partying former team-mate Frank McAvennie, we bumped into Fergie, who took one look at Frank and said, 'I thought you were dead!'

Quick as a flash, Frank shot back with, 'Aye, but you didn't send a shirt did you?'

Eventually, there was only so much passive smoking I could do in John Lyall's car, and it was time to get my own. Thankfully, the club had an association with the local Ford dealers, and it was John himself who took me down there to introduce me to his man at the dealership. He told him that I was the club's new left-back and that he should look after me. He certainly did that, and I walked out of there with a Fiesta 1.1 Popular Plus. I absolutely loved it. You just can't imagine Jurgen Klopp heading down to the local Liverpool

Ford dealership and helping his new signing get a car, can you?

John, and the car, certainly helped me settle in at the club, although the players there also did a great job of that. But let's not forget that John had put together that fine squad.

Billy Bonds was Mr West Ham. Although he was getting to the end of his career, he epitomised everything the club stood for. He was certainly the fittest player I ever played with, both at the time and throughout my career. Alongside Billy were some great characters like Frank McAvennie, Ray Stewart and Alvin Martin, to name a few. A lot of those lads trained the way I was used to at Birmingham so there was no change there, and I clicked with the majority of them straightaway.

Paul Ince was one of the feistiest in training. I know that the West Ham fans were unhappy with the way he left the club, but there was no denying what a good player he was. Paul had a lot of arrogance about him, and was one of those Marmite characters that you either loved or hated. Personally, I love people with a bit of arrogance, as it's an essential ingredient of being a good footballer.

I played against him a few times after he left the club, and he's someone I would definitely prefer to be on my team. He was a winner, very aggressive and a natural box-to-box player. On top of that, he would wind people up on the pitch.

He'd also do that off the pitch with his 'Guvnor' nickname. That's what he called himself. I remember he once said to Liam Brady, a class act on and off the pitch, 'I'm the guvnor here, not you!' I couldn't believe he had the nerve to say that to one of the most experienced players in the dressing room, who had achieved what he had in the game. Liam just responded with a smile, but god knows what he must have been thinking inside. Incey was one of those players that you take, or chuck away.

Playing behind Liam was a joy. He was another fantastic player, who could read the game so well, and we had a natural understanding between us. There wasn't that much discussion on tactics or positioning. If I had to be told what to do, or where to stand, then I wasn't good enough for the team. When Alvin Martin was captain, he'd occasionally yell at me with the odd instruction, but that was it.

The spirit and understanding on the pitch was matched off it, as there was a big social scene. Or, as some would call it, a drinking culture. We would always go out after a game on a Saturday, and that would often lead into further nights out on a Sunday, Monday and Tuesday.

Frank McAvennie had his own routine, as he would often go out to nightclubs with the Page 3 Girls on Thursdays, and sometimes even Friday nights before playing on a Saturday. There was no way that was allowed by the club, but Frank got away with it.

I was happy enough without the showbiz stuff – give me a night out in a pub or club in Basildon or Romford any day of the week. And I never had a problem with going out after we got beat. I remember once going for a drink after we'd been thrashed 4–0 by Southampton. Some of the fans came up to me and asked how we could be going for a drink after such a bad defeat.

'Did you go to the game?' I asked.

'Yeah.'

'Can you question my work rate, passion and pride?'

'No'

'Well there you go, so I'm having a drink.'

I'm a very black and white kind of guy, and that's how I saw it. If I've given it everything I could at work, then I can go out and have a drink after. Why should the result make any difference?

To be honest, when I first started at Birmingham City, I was more concerned with getting decent kit than going out drinking after the game. Not many players had agents at that time, and I certainly didn't, so it was hard to get hold of the best boots. Patrick used to provide Birmingham with a load of kit back then – I'm talking about the sports manufacturing brand, not some Irish fella – and their boots were great, but Nike's and Puma's were quality. Some of the older pros had boot deals, so I used to ask them to sort me out with an extra pair now and again.

And then there was the actual matchday kit. These days, most players get two shirts for every game, one to wear in each half. When I was at West Ham, I would have been lucky to get two shirts for the whole season! Don't get me wrong, I loved coming into training and to games, to find my kit and boots all laid out for me in the changing room. But I always found the neckline of the shirt way too tight for me.

So before every game, I cut the top so I had a bit more breathing room. The problem for Eddie Gillam, the kit man, was that he couldn't just replace the shirt with a new one as there weren't unlimited shirts in those days. Instead, he'd get his poor wife to sew it up, all ready for me to cut it again before the following match.

It was the same with socks – although I didn't cut those up, at least not my own, as sometimes we cut up each other's clothes for a laugh. I loved the feeling of pulling on a new pair of socks for every game, so I told Eddie that would be my preference, to which he replied, 'You ain't gonna get that 'ere, son!'

While kit men like Eddie tended to stick around for years and years, managers never lasted as long. Although John Lyall had been in the West Ham hot seat for what seemed like forever, a little over a year after I joined, he was shown the exit after we were relegated from the top flight. He'd been at the club for 34 years as both player and manager, but that was it. Football is brutal, never more so than in those situations, and I was gutted to see John go, mainly because I'd signed to play for him.

We were all intrigued to see who would replace John after all those years in charge, so when Lou Macari was announced, it's fair to say he was always going to face an uphill task in filling John's shoes.

You have to remember that Lou was West Ham's sixth ever manager. That's right, only five men had been in charge of the club before him for the best part of 90 years of history. So when he questioned my weight in our first meeting, I was already on the back foot and thinking that this isn't going to go very well.

I wasn't the only player to feel that Lou was rubbing people up the wrong way at the club. Yes, we might all have been missing John Lyall, as is very common when a popular manager leaves, but Lou was probably not the best man-manager.

Ultimately, he tried to change too much, too quickly, most notably our style of play. West Ham had always played a certain way and the fans expected us to play proper football. Lou wanted us to be a little bit more direct and get the ball forward quicker. In other words, he expected us to play long ball. But we had a team with Tony Cottee, Frank McAvennie, Alan Devonshire, Ray Stewart and Liam Brady. Did he really think we were going to smash the ball over Brady's head and expect him to support the strikers? The truth is we just didn't listen to those instructions and tried to play the way we knew, the West Ham way.

As I've already said, however, I have a lot to be thankful for to Lou, as he gave me so much during his short time at

Upton Park, including making me captain, free-kick and penalty-taker, and encouraging me to go up for corners.

He also gave me the chance to go head-to-head with him on the football pitch, as he always insisted on joining in with our five-a-side games every Friday at Chadwell Heath. Although I really don't think it's a good idea for a manager to be playing against his own players, because of the risks of causing or receiving an injury, I absolutely loved those games.

Lou would always be on the opposite side to me, maybe because he fancied going up against me, or maybe because he was just daft. Whatever the reason, every Friday I would absolutely fucking nail him. Every time he got the ball, I would batter him. The other lads found it really funny, and to his credit, he would always get up and carry on, demanding the ball again, only for the whole thing to be repeated.

Amazingly, he would never shirk a challenge. Week after week, he'd put himself on the other side to me, and I would never hold back. There were brick walls in the gym we played in, and one week, I absolutely nailed him into one of those walls. He hit the deck, but up he got and carried on. Unbelievable.

There was another game where I went right through him, and genuinely thought I'd broken his leg. He had to be helped to the physio room for treatment, but thankfully there was no lasting damage done.

It was a ridiculous situation. He was the manager, and I wanted to prove a point, so we would always go at it. It's exactly why I think it's such a bad idea for a manager to get involved like that, but the other players loved it.

I always felt that Lou wanted to wind me up, in a way that I never felt any other manager that I played for would have done. I saw him years later, and asked him why he'd often spoken to me in that way, and he said, 'I just wanted a reaction out of you, you played better when you were angry.'

'I'm always fucking angry!' I replied. 'I didn't need help from you!'

Lou was eventually forced to resign after less than a year at the club because of some problems he'd had with his former team Swindon, which meant that Billy Bonds took over. From five managers in 90 years, to two in eight months!

With my former team-mate in charge, our relationship was never straightforward. Don't get me wrong, I had enormous respect for Bill, and he was and will always be a West Ham icon. But, as I might have mentioned already, he was something of a fitness freak, which pissed me right off. On top of that, I was never one to hold back so we'd often have very frank exchanges of views.

Things changed a bit when Billy brought Harry in as his assistant. To my absolute delight, Harry was not completely on-board with Billy's run-til-you-drop training philosophy. Instead, the training was less about running and more about keep-ball sessions, five-a-sides, or shadow play. And all of those will get you fit without running endless laps of the pitch with no ball in sight.

Harry was also good to be around, very popular with the players, and it was obvious he knew what he was doing in those training sessions. He also knew what he was doing in terms of how to manage the players, and make each of us feel special. Although that was only the case if he wanted you.

A manager who definitely wanted me was Liverpool's Graeme Souness. He'd first tried to sign me when I was at Birmingham City, to take me up to Glasgow Rangers, but Garry Pendrey wouldn't let me go at that particular moment. A few years later, the stars had finally aligned and we were able to meet to discuss a different move up north, although I was still very unsure about leaving West Ham. But when I met up with Graeme, as soon as we started chatting, I knew I wanted to sign for him – like I said, I always signed for managers, not clubs. He told me how he needed to add a bit of steel to his side, and with Neil Ruddock already in the back line, he thought I would slot in well.

He was quite similar to Billy Bonds in the way he saw the game. There were no grey areas, black was black, and white was white. You do your job, get paid, and go home. The difference, of course, was that the expectations were enormous. I was at West Ham where we were struggling near the bottom in our first season back in the top flight – at Liverpool, if you didn't win the league, or at least a trophy, that was considered a failure.

But Graeme's no-nonsense approach appealed to me and with the deal seemingly already set up, I realised that I didn't have much choice anyway. Despite not really wanting to leave West Ham, I was on my way to Liverpool. I loved playing under Graeme as he was true to his word, and we were all treated like adults. Before away games, he might join us for a drink in the hotel and tell us stories from the past. And when a bloke who's won everything there is to win in football tells you stories, you listen.

Unfortunately, the results weren't good enough and everything changed for me when Roy Evans took over after Graeme was dismissed. He didn't fancy me as a player, and suddenly I was out of the side, training with the youth team.

I don't know if Harry was keeping tabs on my situation through his son, who was playing at Liverpool, but it was Jamie who came to my rescue one day when he told me that his dad wanted me to come back to West Ham. I told Jamie to tell Harry that I would walk down there.

From a practical point of view, it wasn't ideal, as I had a beautiful house up there and my twin girls had settled in a lovely little village school. But they were very young so it was easier to move them at that time than if they'd been teen-agers, for example. Plus, in football, the costs of uprooting your family are all covered by transfers, so I didn't have to fork out for the removal or anything like that.

When I'd left Upton Park, Billy had still been in charge, but this time not only was Harry organising the transfer, but he was also in the gaffer's seat. I'd heard rumours that Harry had stitched Billy up to get the top job, which Harry denied, but Bill would never talk about what happened. I think Harry convinced the chairman that in order for the club to go to the next level, he needed to be in charge.

Whatever happened, Harry was in the hot seat when I returned and it was great to be back playing for him. He wanted me, and he did a great job of making sure I knew that. He'd always talk to me, and all the other players, about how good we were, and how he could make sure he got the best out of us. His man management skills were right up there, although he could certainly let us have it as well, if need be.

Following a 4–0 defeat by Southampton, we traipsed back into the dressing room. Don Hutchison saw that there was a plate of salmon sandwiches on the physio bed, and was not impressed.

'Fucking salmon sandwiches, what the fuck's this?' he moaned.

'Fucking salmon sandwiches?' yelled Harry, as he picked up the plate and hurled it against the wall, with the sarnies flying all over the changing room.

He could definitely lose his rag, but those were the exceptions to the norm. More usually Harry was a mellow guy, keeping everyone happy. Like Graeme, he would also sit and have a drink with us, and tell us stories about the old days, but he knew where the line was – a manager can't be a player's friend. He can sit down and have a drink with the lads if we're travelling together before a game, but he can't go out and socialise with the team.

In Harry's day, they'd all have a drink before a game on a Friday night. That would never have been officially allowed in our day, although we did get up to all sorts in the hotel the night before a match. He also told us how all the players would smoke in the dressing room at half-time. So the manager might be having a go at them, and they'd all be puffing away on their fags!

Funnily enough, my final experience in football wasn't too dissimilar to those times, as it was in non-league with Canvey Island, which was run by the charismatic nightclub and arcade millionaire Jeff King, who knew my agent Rachel Anderson. Glenn Pennyfather, who had played for Southend and Palace, was the Canvey manager, but Jeff oversaw everything, so it was like having two old-school gaffers at the same time.

Ok, so we weren't all smoking at half-time, but that real raw, grassroots atmosphere of non-league was far closer to the game in the days of Harry and Bobby Moore, than the Premier League I played in until I was forced to retire in 1999.

I absolutely loved playing for Jeff and Glenn. To be fair, Glenn didn't have to say much to any of us because we could all play. Even the lads that were working during the week knew exactly what they were doing so we'd just go out there and do our thing. Training was on Tuesday and Thursday, with a game on Saturday which suited me and my dodgy knee just fine, plus I got on really well with everyone there.

Jeff wasn't afraid of splashing the cash, and he got players in like Steve Tilson, who'd been at Southend but was happy to drop down a league because he was being paid more.

Obviously, playing at that level meant that there were players trying to wind me up every time I stepped out on the pitch, but back then football was still a contact sport. At that level, you get more benefit of the doubt for mistimed tackles and things like that. During my time at Canvey, we enjoyed a fantastic cup run and we beat Northampton, who had Marco Gabbiadini up front. He was trying to wind me up so I just went through him, even after the ball had already gone, but nobody seemed to care.

We also beat Wigan away from home, who had Paul Dalglish playing opposite me, watched by his dad Kenny in the stands. I made sure I kicked him all over the park. Every time he got the ball, I was there, nailing him. It was insane. After the game, which we won 1–0, he came over to me and asked me why I kept kicking him all night, so I replied 'because I was getting away with it.'

It was a huge result for a club like Canvey, and Jeff was absolutely buzzing. We drew Burnley away next but my knee had started playing up again by then so I missed that one. Unfortunately, it was the end of the road for us as we got beat 4–1.

It was an unexpected and amazing experience, a fantastic little swansong to my career, made all the more enjoyable by a great bunch of lads and people who ran the club. As soon as I met Jeff, I knew I wanted to play for him, like all the other top gaffers in my career.

●

I close the car door behind me and look around – where the fuck am I?

All the way here, I've been wondering what to expect, but now I'm looking at a tiny little place with a few Portakabins dotted around.

This is Chadwell Heath, West Ham's no frills training ground. I think I might already love the place.

I walk towards one of those makeshift buildings which hosts a dressing room, and there are a few lads in there already changed and heading out to train.

'Hello,' I hear a few times, as a few of the boys walk past me. 'Hello,' I hear myself saying back. This is all very strange. And new. And different. But yet somehow so familiar.

Despite it being new and strange and different, it also feels like home. Everyone's friendly, warm and welcoming. Not just the players but other people working here as well.

There's Charlie on the gate. I can tell straight away he's proper salt of the earth, and very much part of the furniture here. There's Eddie the kit man, asking me what I need, offering me help.

And then, of course, there's John. John Lyall. The gaffer. The man who's been here forever. The man who's just picked me up from my hotel and given me a lift to training, as if I was a kid playing for a Saturday morning team.

I get changed. I'm wearing West Ham training kit now, because I'm a West Ham player. Birmingham is in the past. Well, that was yesterday. But now it's Thursday, and I'm a Hammer.

I haven't actually signed yet, but that's a formality. I leave the Portakabin, and jog out to the pitches to join my new team-mates.

We train, and I love it even more. This is just like Birmingham. Nobody is holding back, not least me. I'm flying into tackles, maybe giving it even more than I usually would. After all, I need the lads to see what I'm all about, and first impressions last.

There's no doubt I'm giving the best possible impression of what my game is all about. But I can also see that there are players here who are cut from the same cloth as me. We play aggressively and we play to win, whether it's a league game or a keep-ball session in training.

I'm feeling really good about this move now, even better than I did when I first met John. Because now I've got a very small taste of what West Ham is all about, and I haven't even played a game for the club yet.

After hating my previous experience of playing at Upton Park, I'm looking forward to playing there as a home ground.

But that's not going to happen just yet, as I've got a suspension hanging over me so I can't play on Saturday. Nobody has mentioned that yet, but I assume they all know.

I'm walking off the training pitch and, as I head back to the changing room, John tells me to come into his office to sign the contract.

I shower and change, and there's a lot of noise around me. Players are joking around, laughing, bantering. Again, this is like Birmingham, and it makes me feel like I'm at home.

And I'm a part of it straightaway, part of the jokes and the banter, part of the furniture already. That feels good. I'm a West Ham player.

I head out of the Portakabin, and straight into another one, which is John's office. It's time to officially become a West Ham player.

Unsurprisingly, I'm hit by a wall of smoke as I sit down behind his desk. He says something about training, as he hands me the contract, but I'm not really concentrating and say 'yeah' as I look at the papers he's handed me.

I'm not that bothered by what it says. We've already shaken hands on the deal when John came to Birmingham and that's more than good enough for me.

He uses the hand holding his cigarette to point to where I need to sign the contract, and a bit of fag ash falls on to the piece of paper, which he quickly brushes away.

I pick up the pen that's on the table in front of me, and sign my name in the spaces where I need to.

Julian Dicks.

Julian Dicks.

Julian Dicks.

That's it. Job done. I'm a West Ham player. But I don't think I needed to sign my name on the dotted line to know that.

Either way, this feels good, sitting in John's office, knowing that everything is sorted, and I can now get on with playing. Except I'm suspended.

While I'm thinking this, John's talking to me about the club, telling me about some more of the history, about Upton Park, the East End, the community, Bobby Moore, Geoff Hurst, Martin Peters.

What a club, and what a history, and now I'm going to be a part of it.

And then he suddenly says: 'Do you know you're suspended for Saturday?'

My heart kind of sinks a bit, as I say 'yeah'.

'I fucking didn't, otherwise I wouldn't have signed you!'

I'm half-shocked, but half-laughing with him, as he seems to be smiling at me. Hopefully, he's joking.

He's got other stuff to do so I head out of his office, leaving him to it.

Man United at home would have been a pretty good debut, but I'm going to have to sit that one out. But I'm raring to go. I could play a game right now, despite having just trained.

HAMMER TIME

I head into the gym and kick a ball around. It's all I know, and all I've ever known. I was born to do this and, hopefully, I was born to play for West Ham. I can't wait to find out.

THE HARD MEN

The elbow and the missing teeth

This is just like old times, and I'm really enjoying it.

It's a hell of a challenge, but I'm giving it everything I've got.

I'm patrolling the left side of our half at Kenilworth Road. Somewhere to my right is Luton striker Mick Harford, and we've just become reacquainted from our Birmingham days.

Neither of us is holding back, just like how we used to train at Birmingham a few years back. I can still feel the effect of one of Mick's very pointy elbows in my ribs, from when we were fighting for the ball just a minute ago.

I've got no problem with it, this is how the game is played. It won't be long before I'll have a chance to get him back.

This is the first time I've played here and the ground is tight, a bit like Upton Park with the fans within touching distance. I like it.

We get a corner, so I bomb forward into the penalty area which the gaffer has been encouraging me to do. I'm jostling for position in the box, and I can see Mick keeping an eye on me. They know I'm a threat in the air, despite being only 5 ft 10.

I look at Mick, and look up. I have to do that because he's 6 ft 4. A fucking massive bloke but not exactly a tank, because he's so slim.

I keep my eye on the corner, as the ball swings in. I make a run, but it's an inswinger so I'm not going to get close to it. Mick's running alongside me, but we both watch the goal-keeper claim the ball comfortably, and I start jogging back to my own half.

I look along the line as the keeper prepares to punt it forward. We're a solid bank of four, just as we should be.

The ball comes flying towards the halfway line where it's met firmly by the head of one of our centre-halves. And then it's headed just as firmly back in my direction, so I bring it down and play a pass forwards.

I follow the ball, as we try to build an attack, while keeping an eye on my opposite number who's got some defending to do. I look round and see Mick prowling around the halfway line, waiting to feed off any scraps that might come his way, like the proper old fashioned centre-forward that he is.

Our attack breaks down and the ball is played forward, but it's too long and our keeper gathers it. His goal kick is high and heading towards me, so I adjust my feet, walk back a bit.

Mick's moving towards me, I can see him from my left. He wants his head on this ball too. But I can flick this on. I think I'll get there before him.

The ball's about to drop, and Mick's getting closer now, so

I ready myself to flick it with the back of my head, jumping to meet it.

Mick leaps at the same time with his arm out, and his head reaches the ball just before mine does, and his pointy elbow also reaches my face.

BANG!

For fuck's sake, Mick.

I look up and can see Mick running off after the ball. Why the fuck did he do that?

I run back towards our penalty area. I've got some defending to do.

My eye feels like it's closing. I can feel some swelling as I touch it. It's not in a good state but I can see, so I can play. I can't work out how he won that ball. But I definitely know why my eye's half-shut. The cheeky fucker.

The game moves to their half, so I get forward in support – thankfully, I've got no defending to do right now.

I hear a whistle and look at the referee. It's half-time. Thank fuck for that. Everyone walks towards the changing rooms, and I follow. I touch the area around my eye again and it feels even bigger, like a tennis ball or something.

'What happened to you?' says a voice next to me.

I look round and it's Mick. He's not smiling, he looks serious.

'You fucking elbowed me!' I reply.

'Did I?' he says, looking genuinely puzzled.

'Yeah, you did. Did you mean it?'

'No, I definitely didn't,' he says, and pats me on the shoulder.

We're off the pitch now, so he goes into his dressing room and I head to mine.

I think I believe him, but I'm not happy. I touch my hand to my eye again, and it feels like someone's stuck a balloon on my face. I'm in the dressing room, and the physio's looking at my eye.

'I'm not coming off,' I tell him, just in case he's even thinking of suggesting something stupid like that. 'I can see fine,' I say, showing him that my eye's open so there's no drama there.

I don't tell him how much it hurts, because I need to get out there for the second half.

I'd have to be dead to miss that.

•

It turned out that Mick had cracked my eye socket in four places. I played the rest of the game and by full-time, it felt like I had my own football on the side of my face to take home with me – without even scoring a hat-trick.

There were a lot of tough, no-nonsense players in the era in which I played, but Mick Harford stands out for me as being head and shoulders above the rest. And not just because he was 6 ft 4.

Mick was very strong, and an extremely physical and aggressive player, but alongside all that, or maybe even because of that, he was an outstanding centre-forward and a superb footballer.

He was definitely a player you wanted with you on your side, and I was fortunate that happened at Birmingham, although that was only for a short time. Mick also scored loads of goals wherever he went, showing there was a lot more to his game than just the physical side of it.

The other player who I probably found the toughest to play against was Mark Hughes, who often gets overlooked when it comes to the physical players of that time. Mark wasn't necessarily a hard bastard like Mick was, but he was as strong as a bull. Sometimes, I'd make a tough challenge and would just bounce straight back off him. He had legs like a pair of tree trunks.

And he certainly didn't mind the physical side of it either. He'd just dust himself down and would then let me have it the next time, which is how I love the game to be played. No moaning, just get on with it. And, of course, he was another player who smashed in hundreds of goals as well, so there was a lot more to his game.

A lot of people talk about Duncan Ferguson when it comes to the hardest players at that time, and I'm sure he was a tough nut but we never had any major issues on the pitch. I know that he had a few rows with other players, but I think a lot of that stemmed from the same frustration that I had, in terms of the people who were happy to dish it out on the pitch but would then piss and moan if they were on the receiving end.

I never had a problem with the way Duncan played. I remember one game against Everton towards the end of my Hammers career, when he absolutely battered a very young Rio Ferdinand all over the park. I think that's when Rio might have realised that he had to get a lot more physical to succeed, and it would certainly have been an experience he would have learned so much from.

Ferguson was a great player, and he would walk all over you if you let him. I was always of the opinion that you had to stand up to players like that and show them that you weren't going to be intimidated or scared of them. If that meant giving them a kick here and there, then so be it. In a weird way, physical players respected anyone who might be prepared to mix it with them – but you did that at your own risk.

Later in my career, Arsenal's Patrick Vieira emerged as an incredible all-round mix of skill, ability and aggression. He was a fantastic player, who stood well over 6 ft tall and was super aggressive. If it went off on the pitch, he'd always be involved, standing his ground, defending his team-mates. And he was part of a truly incredible team.

That Arsenal side were on a completely different level and were so difficult to play against. Just trying to get near them was hard enough for me, never mind kick any of them. They were certainly not afraid to mix it whenever it was needed, a lot like Stuart Pearce who eventually replaced me as left-back at West Ham. He was the England left-back for many years, and some people thought he was keeping me out of the team, but I'm not so sure I was ever being considered given some of my early run-ins with Dave Sexton in the Under-21s.

Stuart was a really aggressive player, another one with massive legs on him. He was tough, and completely uncompromising. He would go straight through you without even thinking about it.

Mark Dennis was another superb left-back of that time, who never got the recognition he deserved, mainly because of his reputation in my opinion. He did win three England Under-21 caps, but he was easily good enough to have played for the senior team.

When I started at Birmingham, I played as a number ten and Mark was the left-back. I really looked up to him and loved his attitude which was care-free to say the least. The bloke did not give a shit and was a bit of a loon. He would kick and punch you off the ball, and that was just in training. As I said before, with only one camera filming games in the eighties and early nineties, it was easy for players to leave their mark on opponents once the ball was at the other end of the pitch.

Like myself, when it came to the action on the pitch in front of the referee, I don't think Mark ever set out to hurt anybody. In the heat of the battle, tackles would often get mistimed, and that's when the yellow or red cards would come out. And on that front, Mark even outdid me, as he was sent off 12 times in his career. He knew that much about being shown red cards that when I went through that rough period of being sent off three times in four months, he reached out to me.

When everyone was busy slagging me off at that time, Mark understood exactly what I was going through and he wrote me a letter, telling me to keep going and to not let it get me down because it was just part of the game. It really meant a huge amount to me, and also showed a side of Mark that not many people saw. As much as he could be a bit of a nutter on the pitch, that was just on the pitch. That doesn't mean he was like that off the pitch, and the letter he wrote to me is proof of the caring type of bloke he was.

I think I also suffered from the same kind of reputation problems as Mark, because of all my red cards and the fiery way that I played football. What people didn't understand is that didn't necessarily mean that I was like that off the pitch.

Far too many people were mistaken in making that assumption about me, but ask any of my team-mates, the people that really knew me, and they'd tell you a very different story. But it's very hard to change a reputation once you've got it. It sticks like glue. Years later, when I was applying for managerial jobs in non-league, not only did I not get many of them, but few people even had the decency to get back to me. I found that very frustrating.

Paul Ince was another player I played with, and later against, who earned himself a big reputation. He was a fantastic box-to-box midfielder, as well as a feisty, ballsy little sod. He had incredible belief in his own ability and didn't appear to have any fear.

I remember one training game at Chadwell Heath, where Paul was on the halfway line, dishing out a load of abuse at goalkeeper Alan McKnight. He was absolutely caning poor Alan, who finally had enough, and sprinted the 45 yards from his goal to confront his tormentor. But Paul saw him coming all day long and launched himself into a drop-kick which felled Alan as soon as he arrived on the halfway line. Brutal, but by no means was that the only fight ever to have taken place on the training ground.

There were fisticuffs regularly, as players who were giving their all might fall out over a bad challenge, or some bad feeling. But once it was done, it was over and it was very rare for anything like that to continue beyond the training pitch. There was one incident, however, which did continue way beyond the confines of Chadwell Heath, mainly because it happened in front of the Sky Sports cameras, which was obviously unusual for training. On that occasion, the Sky crew were there to speak to Harry Redknapp after training, and they'd been allowed to get some footage of us to go with the interview.

We were in the middle of a game and, as usual, everyone was training hard. John Moncur played a pass to John Hartson which went about a foot away from him but, for some reason, the big striker didn't bother trying to run for it. Moncs, being the character he is, absolutely hammered him for that, really laying into John for not bothering to make an effort to reach his pass. Nine times out of ten that kind of thing will happen in training, and it'll just be laughed off by the other player. But, on this particular occasion, Hartson saw red.

Little Eyal Berkovic was on the ball by now and, as if to make up for not trying to get to Moncur's pass, Hartson steamed into Berkovic, leaving him in a crumpled heap on the floor. To his credit, big John realised that the red mist had descended and that he'd gone way over the top with his challenge on Berkovic, so he went over to pick him up off the floor and apologise.

But as John bent down to say sorry, Eyal swung a punch at him, still clearly pissed off about the over-the-top challenge. The weird thing was that John then kind of walked away, before swinging his boot out at Berkovic and kicking him right in the face. It all happened so quickly. In the space of a few seconds, John had completely lost the plot.

Harry, who was watching from the sidelines, yelled, 'Johnny, what are you doing?'

And a still steaming Hartson stormed off the pitch and replied, 'And you can fuck off as well!'

Unfortunately for John, with the Sky cameras being there, the incident was all over the TV and newspapers and he became public enemy number one for a little while.

What he did was obviously wrong, but I felt bad for him because these things can happen in the heat of the moment at training, and nobody ever really knows about them. It's usually a case of what happens on the training ground, stays on the training ground.

He ended up getting a three-game ban for the incident, but by then he'd moved to Wimbledon. I was just grateful that the FA weren't regularly dishing out bans for training ground incidents, or I might have never played football.

The same can probably be said for my one-time team-mate and former manager Billy Bonds, who was never one to duck a challenge or fight. As I explained, Billy was one of the only things I knew about West Ham before I signed for them. There were those horrible fans in the Chicken Run, who I would end up loving, John Lyall, and Billy.

During my one game at Upton Park with Birmingham before I moved there permanently, Billy was involved in a clash with Robert Hopkins, our winger. Rob definitely came off second best against Billy's elbow, and I have a very distinct memory of him on his hands and knees on the Upton Park turf, searching for the two front teeth that Billy had knocked clean out of his mouth.

Billy made a huge impression on me that day, and not just because of Rob's teeth. And the more I got to know him when I joined West Ham, the more I realised that if there was one player I would want alongside me if my life depended on it, it would definitely be Billy.

There were probably harder players than Billy to have played the game, but if there were, you could probably count them on one hand. The man would walk through brick walls and he'd play through any kind of pain, whether it was a broken toe, or even a broken leg. Nothing could stop him – without a doubt, he was my favourite player.

Not that I was thinking that during the first game I played for Birmingham at West Ham, with the home fans making a lasting impression on me. The Birmingham supporters I played in front of were also fierce, but I think the only fans who came close to creating the kind of intimidating atmosphere you got at Upton Park were Millwall's.

I'm well aware there's no love lost between the Hammers and the Lions, and I found that out the hard way when I played at The Den. We were defending a corner and I was standing near the goal waiting for it to be taken when I felt something hard hit me on the arm. I looked down and there was half a house brick lying on the pitch next to me.

These days, a game would be stopped if something like that happened. Back then, I rolled the brick off the pitch then did my best to defend the corner. We won 1–0 that night, and at the final whistle all the players went down to the away end to clap our fans, who were obviously in great voice and spirits with the victory.

Unfortunately, the same couldn't be said for the home fans, who made sure we had to be escorted off the pitch by riot police who raised their shields over our heads to protect us from all the stuff that was raining down on us from the stands as we left the pitch.

I once played at The Den in a testimonial for Millwall legend Les Briley, and I got the most unbelievable amount of abuse from the home fans. Even at a testimonial! I have to admit that I loved playing at Millwall, because I relished the intimidating and fiery atmosphere. I thrived on it, actually.

Give me an intense atmosphere and some physically imposing opposition who are up for the fight, and I'm anyone's. If anything, that would play right into my hands, because I'm not afraid of a battle.

What was much harder for me were the tricky wingers I came up against who were incredibly skilful and faster than the speed of light. Or so it seemed to me.

The quickest of them all was Franz Carr, of Nottingham Forest and Newcastle fame. He was insanely fast. Playing against him was a nightmare for me and, as I already mentioned earlier, my frustration once got the better of me when I elbowed him and was sent off.

As well as Carr, there was Ruel Fox of Norwich and later Newcastle and Spurs, and Tony Daley of Villa. Without a doubt, they were the three hardest wingers I faced and gave me the most difficulty with their pace.

The only way to deal with them was to get physical as soon as possible in the game. Even the managers would tell me to put them in the stands in the first five minutes. If I ever managed to do that, I knew I'd have an easier day as a result, because I'd have landed an important physical and psychological blow.

The problem with Franz Carr was that he didn't care how many times I kicked him, he'd tear me a new arsehole on the pitch time and time again.

The other problem with the speedy wide men was the ball over the top. If that happened, I was taken out of the game, as there was no way I was going to make up the ground to even make a challenge. In those circumstances, the left centre-back would come across to cover and bail me out, in theory. In practice, that man was Tony Gale when I was first playing at West Ham, and I don't remember him ever once doing that.

Most of those tricky, skilful players wanted the ball to feet anyway, which actually suited me far better, because then I could show them inside, which made it far harder for them to be effective and helped me win the duel.

One tactic I hardly ever employed with the wingers was intimidation through verbals. Whether it was on the pitch, or in the tunnel before a game, I always kept quiet and would never start eyeballing anyone, or anything like that. Although there was one notable exception, when I was playing in a reserve game at Highbury for West Ham against Arsenal.

I've no idea why I did this – maybe because it wasn't a first-team game, or it might have been because I absolutely loved playing at Highbury – but I was captaining the Hammers side that day, and as I walked past the Gunners

winger Anders Limpar near the changing rooms, I decided
to wind him up.

'I'm gonna smash you all around Highbury,' I told him.

'Who, me?' he asked with a confused look on his face.

'Yeah, you!'

'Not a chance,' he said, confidently.

'Let me tell you, you come near me, and I'm gonna
smash you in the stands,' I said, before I walked off.

Once we were out on the pitch, I can honestly say that
from the first whistle to the last, Limpar never came within
five yards of me for the entire game. I found it hilarious that
my crap attempt at intimidation actually worked.

Looking back, maybe I should've tried that more often,
but it just wasn't my style. More often than not, I was one of
those players who did his talking on the pitch.

•

*I grab a couple of empty pint glasses, and stick them on top
of the dirty plates that I was already carrying, and head back
into the kitchen.*

*I stick the glasses on the tray with the others that are
going to be washed, and scrape the food remains off the plates
into the bin.*

*I go back out to the bar area and pick up a few more
empty glasses, then take them into the kitchen.*

*Then I head back out but this time I'm behind the bar,
where there's a punter waiting to be served.*

'What can I get you mate?'

'Pint of Stella, and a G&T please,' he says.

I take a fresh pint glass from the stack and stick it under the Stella tap, holding it at an angle until the beer is almost full to the top, and there's no huge frothy head which nobody really wants.

I flip round, take a glass from above the bar, and stick that into the gin dispenser, before pulling a bottle of tonic water out of the fridge and pouring it in the glass.

'There you go, mate,' I say as I put both drinks in front of him on the bar.

I ring up the drinks on the cash till.

'That'll be £6.20 please.'

'Here you go,' says the bloke, handing me a tenner.

I stick it in the till, and give him his change.

He's looking at me quite intently. I think he's recognised me. This happens a lot, and the truth is I love it.

Since I stopped playing, one of the things I miss the most is the fans. They were the ones I played for, as well as for myself of course. I almost took for granted those occasions when I would chat with fans, sign autographs and all that.

This is now the next best thing. The Shepherd and Dog may not be Upton Park on a Saturday afternoon, but it certainly keeps me busy.

The bloke takes his drinks over to his table, where his missus is sitting. I presume it's his missus, I have no idea really.

I walk over to the side of the bar to pick up some glasses that I've just noticed have been left there. As I walk back towards the kitchen, I can feel my knee. I haven't played football for more than a year, and that was for Canvey Island, yet I still get a bit of pain there.

Standing on my feet for ten hours at a time is probably not doing it any favours, but this is my job now.

There's no sugar-coating it. It's fucked. That's why I'm not playing any kind of football now, even though I'm 33.

There are plenty of lucky bastards still playing at a decent level, former team-mates of mine. I hope they appreciate what they've got.

I give my knee a rub. For no particular reason as that's not going to make any difference to the damage inside it. As I do that, I see the guy who just bought the drinks coming back over to the bar. Is he going to talk football with me? I'd imagine he is. They usually do. And I'm always happy to oblige.

'Can I order some food please?' he says.

'Sure, here's the menu,' I reply, handing it to him. Then I add, 'We also have our specials on the board there,' while pointing to the chalk board on the wall.

He looks over to the board, then back at the menu, while I stand there waiting to take his order.

Eventually, he looks up and says: 'I used to watch you play.'

I knew it.

'Oh yeah?' I reply, smiling at him.

'You were a bit feisty weren't you!'

'Just a bit,' I say, as he chuckles to himself.

He tells me he's an Arsenal fan, and remembers me getting sent off at Highbury for a foul on Ian Wright.

'That was never a second yellow. Wrighty made the most of that, and I told him as much when he came to West Ham,' I say, because it's still important to me for people to hear my side of these stories. It always will be.

We carry on chatting about football, talking about players he liked to watch and the ones I played alongside. Eventually, he orders a steak and a burger.

'I've got to say, you're nothing like I imagined you to be,' he says.

'I hope that's in a good way,' I reply.

'I thought you were a right nutter!' he says.

'Yeah, that was just me on the pitch.'

It's not the first time I've had that kind of conversation and I'm sure it won't be the last.

He sits back down, and there are a couple of blokes waiting to be served at the bar. I take care of their drinks, and then head into the kitchen. I look up at the clock, and realise there's still a long evening ahead, but I'm looking forward to it.

Running this place gives me an enormous amount of satisfaction. I've always loved pubs, obviously, so to get the chance to own one was a bit of a dream. I know that it's a cliché as an ex-footballer to buy a pub, but out here in Essex, *we're in a beautiful part of the country, and I take great pride in my work just like I did when I was a footballer.*

The door opens and a couple of blokes walk in. They look at me, and big smiles appear on their faces.

'Alright Julian?' says one of them.

'Hello mate, what can I get you?' I reply.

I don't know the bloke, but no doubt these are football fans who have come in for a drink and a chat. I'm very happy to help with both.

'Two pints please, and whatever you're having,' says the man.

I could probably do with a glass of something to keep my mind off my knee, so I take him up on his offer.

'That's very kind of you,' I say. 'You from round here?'

'Nah, just passing through. We heard you ran the place, so wanted to come in for a pint.'

'Hammers fans?'

'Spurs!' says the other bloke.

'Ok then,' I say, smiling at them, knowing how little time West Ham fans have for Tottenham.

I get their drinks, pour myself a glass of red wine, as we talk football. They're remembering matches, and it doesn't take long before we're discussing West Ham's epic 4–3 win over Spurs from a few years back. It's one of my favourite games as I scored two goals and made one for John Hartson. And, well, we beat Tottenham which was always special for us and the supporters.

And now I'm laughing about it with a couple of Spurs fans. That certainly wouldn't have happened a few years ago.

We exchange a bit of banter about the game, as we all sip our drinks. They're not shy to point out that I was a bit lively on the pitch.

'The truth is I never set out to hurt anyone,' I say, a line I've said many times before, and it is totally authentic. 'It was just the way I played.'

They give me some stick about the John Spencer incident. It's nothing I've not heard a thousand times before, but I protest my innocence as always.

'I tell you what,' I say to them. 'I could've played for Tottenham.'

'No way,' they say, almost in unison.

'Yeah, Ossie Ardiles tried to sign me when I was at Liverpool. Straight up.'

'What happened?' one of them asks, while draining his pint.

So, I tell them.

'Roy Evans was making me train with the kids at the time, which I was pissed off about. I just wanted to play football, not piss about with 16 and 17-year-olds.

'He called me into his office and told me that Birmingham wanted to take me on loan, but I wasn't interested in a loan move. I had a wife and two kids living up near Liverpool, I was 25 or 26 years old, so the last thing I wanted was to be going anywhere on a temporary basis.

'Then he called me in again a while later and said Tottenham wanted me. I said, "Fuck off!"'

'And he said, "No, seriously, they want you."'

'So I said, "Seriously, fuck off!"'

'So Roy says, "What do you mean?"'

'"West Ham and Spurs don't mix," I told him. "It just doesn't work."'

'And he says again, "Seriously?"'

'So I explained to him that I have principles, and that if I signed for Tottenham, there is no way that the West Ham fans would ever forgive me. I just can't do that to them.'

The blokes are looking at me like I've just told them they've lost a close relative.

'That's unbelievable,' says one of them. 'But fair play to you.'

I finish my wine, and then head off to take some more food orders from some customers who have just arrived. The place is starting to fill up which I always love to see. I look around and I can only see a handful of empty tables. Happy days.

I go back to the bar where the Spurs fans are still seated, empty pint glasses in front of them.

'Another pint, gents?' I say.

'Go on then, you twisted my arm,' laughs one of them.

'You know what,' says the other man as I'm pouring their pints. 'I hated you as a West Ham player, absolutely hated you. But I'm sure I would've loved you if you'd played for Tottenham.'

I smile to myself, as I hand them their drinks. I may not have won any major trophies in my career, but I realise that I won something else. I won the fans over.

For all the 20-goal-a-season strikers there are, deep down maybe supporters are just looking for whole-hearted players who give everything for the cause on the pitch. And chuck in the odd elbow or kick at a rival player.

'Thank you,' I say, handing over the drinks. 'That's very kind, but there is no way in the world I would ever have played for Spurs.'

THE CAPTAIN

Pre-match. The Tunnel. The Refs

I hate this bit. It's total bollocks but it has to be done.

The gaffer gives me the teamsheet, and off I go.

I couldn't be prouder to be the captain of West Ham. I absolutely love putting the armband on my sleeve. But this is definitely the downside of it, and I can actually feel my mood darkening right now.

I walk out of the dressing room, followed by the gaffer's assistant. We turn right, then left, then knock on a door with a sign on it saying 'Referee'.

Yes, it's that time of the week again, when I get to be lectured by some bloke dressed in a black top and shorts, flanked by his two linesmen, also clad in black.

They come up with the same crap every week, I really cannot see the point of it at all.

Like clockwork, my opposite number has joined us, with his assistant manager alongside him too. We must all be gluttons for punishment.

I nod at them both, and say hello, but inside I'm thinking I just want to get into my pre-match bath. I decide to try to keep my mind focused on the Cokes and Mars bar, to help get through this.

The door opens, and we're all invited in. It's not a massive space, so it already feels awkward and nobody has even started speaking yet.

I look down at the teamsheet and scan the names: Miklosko, Potts, Dicks, Gale, Martin, Keen, Brady, Slater, Quinn, Allen, Ward.

I look up and the referee is staring at me, with his hand out, as if he wants me to give him a pre-match tip or something.

Then something clicks in my brain. He wants the teamsheet. That shows me how much I've already switched off, just from having to do this.

I hand it over to him, and he starts talking, but I'm finding it hard to focus.

He's telling us what we can't do on the pitch, what will get us bookings, and what he doesn't want to see or hear. I wonder if he's aware that today isn't the first time any of us have played football.

I look over to the other skipper, and his eyes have glazed over in the same way that mine probably have.

Focus on the Cokes and Mars, I tell myself as the ref keeps talking, but this feels never ending. This is not what I signed up for.

I wonder if anyone ever listens to the refs at these pre-match gatherings. I've yet to meet anyone who thinks they're a good idea.

As he continues to speak, the bath, Cokes and Mars feel further away than ever. What the fuck am I doing here?

As I'm thinking, I'm looking down on the floor. I'm so bored, I can't even think about anything anymore, other than getting out of here. I just want to play football, not do any of this bollocks.

I look up, and the ref has stuck his hand out again. What now? I've already given him the teamsheet.

'Good luck!' he says to me, with his hand still sticking out.

Oh, right! I think we're done. I shake his hand, and then shake everyone else's hand in there. Suddenly, there's a lot of hand-shaking going on.

But then the door opens, and we all file out of there, as quickly as possible – at least that's what I do.

The door shuts behind us, and I turn to the oppo's captain and say 'what a sack of shit that was!'

He laughs and agrees, then heads off towards the away dressing room while I go around the corner, back to ours. Time for a bath.

•

The buzzer in the dressing room goes. That's it. It's time.

The pre-match bath is done, the Cokes and Mars are also done, and I'm ready to go.

I look around the dressing room, and everyone's off the benches and on to their feet.

'Right boys . . .' says the gaffer, but there's not much point, as there's nothing that can be said right now that will make any difference.

I know what I have to do, we all know what we have to do. If we didn't, then we wouldn't be in here, we'd be up in the stands watching.

I walk to the dressing room door. I feel calm and totally up for this. It would be unusual for me to feel anything else at this point, as I never get pre-match nerves. Today is no exception.

I'm about to open the door, so I check behind me and see that all the lads are standing up and ready to go.

I open the door, and I immediately turn to my right, and hear the clatter of my boots on the floor, and then the same from Ludo's behind me, and on it goes as everyone comes out of the dressing room.

We go past the walls that have loads of Hammers history all over them – Moore, Peters, Hurst, the trophies, the proud heritage of this great club.

I'm not looking at those walls, but I know that they're there, accompanying me and the boys on our journey to the pitch.

I take a left and I can see the light up and ahead in the distance, and I can also see our opponents today, who are already at the end of the tunnel, waiting for us.

We're not deliberately keeping them waiting – their dressing room is closer to the pitch than ours, and they must have walked out on the 'b' of the buzzer.

There's a flight of stairs to climb before we're standing alongside the other team, and then one more flight after that to get to pitch level.

I walk up the first set of stairs, once again hearing the noise of the studs of my boots on each one. I don't leap up them on purpose. I might do that if I was nervous, but my calmness makes me walk up them very easily.

I carry on along the walkway, and now I'm walking past the oppo. I'm not really looking at them as individuals, although there is one that I know from the past, and we nod at each other.

I stop when I'm standing alongside their skipper again, as I was an hour ago in the referee's room. It's not quite as boring this time, as we're both ready to play.

He's looking straight ahead, at the next flight of stairs, and bright light of the stadium in front of us. We're practically standing shoulder to shoulder. Everyone is.

I look round and see all the boys have stopped in a line behind me. Most are staring straight ahead. One or two are jumping up and down on the spot.

Someone yells 'come on lads!' but I can't even tell who it is, one of ours, or theirs.

I can hear the noise outside. The fans are singing, the PA system is blasting out music, there's a proper buzz out there, and we're about to walk straight into it.

These are the moments that make being a footballer so special. I know that, but I can hardly think about that right *now as I'm focused on the game, on doing my job, on doing my very best for West Ham.*

The referee and the linesmen suddenly appear next to me, then walk in front of us. They've made their way through both sets of players.

The ref looks round at me, and everyone behind us, then he looks ahead. He's waiting for the signal from someone to walk up the stairs and on to the pitch.

So we all wait.

The noise in the stadium outside gets louder and louder. The fans are as ready as we are.

Finally, the referee and linesmen start to walk up the stairs, so I follow them.

Again, I climb each stair in a relaxed way, no running or leaping up them, and now I'm at the top, walking into the stadium, across the massive West Ham logo and out on to the pitch.

An enormous roar fills the air as I walk out on to the pitch, followed by my team-mates. Instinctively, I raise my hands above my head and clap the fans, by way of appreciation for their support.

Now I break out into a little jog, while some of the other lads do the same, or some little sprints, or stretches.

I can hear the beginning of the 'Bubbles' song being played in the stadium, and suddenly it's being chanted loudly and proudly. It feels so familiar, part of all of our pre-match build-up, both fans and players.

I can see the referee's in the centre circle now and, as the 'Bubbles' chorus finishes and gives way to chants of 'United! United!' I make my way over there to do the most important job as skipper – flipping a coin.

The referee hands me the 10 pence piece which I lob up into the air, while my opposite number calls 'heads'. The ref bends down, picks it up, and says 'tails' so I choose to stay where we are, giving the other lot kick-off.

There's lots more hand-shaking again, which I only really do in a half-hearted way as I'm now very focused on the game.

I march back to the left-back spot, and look alongside me where my fellow defenders are lined up.

There are a few more claps of hands and shouts, but I can hardly hear them, because the fans are still singing, with the away supporters making plenty of noise too.

I'm focused on winning that first 50-50, getting on the ball, hitting that first pass.

Ahead of me, I watch the referee look around the pitch, then put the whistle to his mouth and blow.

Let's do this.

●

It was always a bit of a relief for me once the match started, as it meant that I could do the only thing I ever wanted to do which was play football. I wasn't a complicated man, all I needed was a football and I'd play. I was exactly the same as a boy too. The only thing I'd ever wanted to do was play football.

Everyone handled those moments before a game in different ways. We all had our own routines, even if mine were quite different to everyone else's in terms of not ever warming up.

My refusal to go on the pitch with the others before a game and hop in the bath instead, was met by resistance from a few managers, but I always won them over in the end because I could be a right stubborn sod when I wanted to be.

Lou Macari banned me from having my Cokes before the game, but that was part of a wider nutrition strategy he tried to implement. Fortunately for us and unfortunately for him, it lasted about as long as he did at Upton Park, which wasn't very long at all.

In many ways, Lou was years ahead of everyone else with his approach as it took at least five or six years for every club to start taking players' diets seriously. It coincided with the large numbers of foreign players who came to play in the Premier League, and brought with them new ideas about what we should all be eating and drinking. But Lou was fighting a losing battle with us lot back in 1989, as we just weren't ready for his changes. If anything, he tried to do too much, too soon, which backfired.

He banned us from having desserts so that when we were staying in a hotel on the Friday night before an away game, he'd make sure we only had our starters and mains. And he was also quite prescriptive about what we ate, as he wanted us to eat more pasta. My pre-match meal was always steak and beans, and I never changed that.

My team-mate Mark Ward wasn't having any of Lou's new ideas though. 'Fuck him,' he said once he'd finished his main, then headed over to the dessert trolley and took the biggest wedge of cake you've ever seen.

'What are you doing?' said Lou.

'Fuck off!' said Wardy. 'It's Friday night!' as he started wolfing it down right in front of the gaffer.

Lou also banned ketchup, much to everyone's dismay. He was consistent as it was all about sugar, which was why he wouldn't let me have my Cokes in the bath before a game. But he extended that to a Friday night as well, so when I ordered two pints of Coke to my hotel room on room service, they never came.

I called room service to find out where the drinks were, and I was told that they'd been asked by the manager not to bring those drinks to my room. I made it very clear to them that they should still bring me my Cokes, never mind what the manager said. After all, what else was I going to have with my Jack Daniel's?

It eventually got to the point where all room service was banned, so I had to smuggle cans of Coke into my bag with me before away games, along with my bottle of Jack, of course. Even with the room service ban, Lou was not satisfied as he'd come and knock on everyone's door to make sure we weren't drinking or getting up to no good. It was all a bit much.

When he left, I went back to my usual pre-match routine, Cokes and all. I appreciate that players wouldn't get away with that now, but I was playing at a very different time, where allowances were made for certain players.

One of those was that it was understood that I didn't do the pre-match warm-up, and I also never did the pre-training warm-up either, although Harry Redknapp tried to put his foot down with that, insisting that I joined in.

It wasn't down to laziness on my part, as I wasn't somebody who just couldn't be arsed to do the warm-up. In fact, I was usually at training an hour before everyone, doing my own shooting and passing practice. It was far more because I knew my own body, and I recognised that I didn't need to do all of those exercises. Except, Harry thought he knew better.

A while after I returned to West Ham from Liverpool and Harry was in sole charge, he told me that I had to join in with the warm-up before training, despite my strong objections. I was the club captain again by then, so he thought I should lead by example, even though I thought everyone needed to do what's right for them. By that stage, the approach to training was changing massively – not only was there a long warm-up, but training finished with a long warm-down too. Bollocks to that.

But Harry was determined that I would join in with all the other players, saying I had to start doing it the very next day.

The following morning, I joined the lads for the warm-up. Harry's assistant Frank Lampard Sr suggested that as I was the captain, I should lead the team on a couple of laps round the pitch. 'Fuck off, that's your job, you take them!' was my response to that ridiculous idea.

I jogged with them, at the back as usual, and we went round the pitch twice, then started to do some stretches. I did them all, every single one, without any complaint. Finally, the ball came out and we started playing some keep ball. The first time I went to kick the ball, I grabbed the back of my leg and yelled at Harry: 'Fuck, I've done my hammy! And it's all because you made me stretch!'

I limped off the training pitch and headed back into the dressing room. It was a performance worthy of an Oscar, but I'd made my point. I might have chucked a moody one, but Harry let me do what I wanted after that in terms of warming up. He was a superb man-manager, so he realised he might have to concede a bit of ground on this one.

I personally believed it had to be a horses for courses approach. I didn't need to warm up. I just didn't. And then you had someone like our right-back Tim Breacker. I think one of his parents might have been an athlete, and Tim used to be a professional warmer-upper. Seriously, he'd start stretching about an hour before everyone else, and he would warm up every part of his body – he'd even stretch his fingers. And yet, he was quite injury-prone with hamstring pulls, quad pulls, all sorts.

I don't think there was one approach that was for everyone, not in terms of training or pre-match warm-ups. It was the same in the dressing room and in the tunnel before the games. There were players who had so much nervous energy that they'd be jumping around the changing room yelling their heads off, so they could stay pumped up. Either that, or once they were in the tunnel, they'd be bouncing around like lunatics. I took a quieter, calmer approach.

If I think about standing in the tunnel now, I can picture Martin Allen foaming at the mouth as he was so eager to get out there. That's exactly why he got the nickname Mad Dog. Ian Bishop would be pissing around with his hair, probably re-tying his ponytail or something.

While all that was going on, some players might have had a chat with the opposition. We used to play the same teams and the same players often, so you'd get to know a lot of the other players, and say hello. We'd also often come up against former team-mates, with whom we might have struck up good friendships, so it would be odd not to acknowledge them.

I'd always say hello to Arsenal's David Rocastle even though he caused me so many problems on the pitch. I never met him outside of football, but we'd always have a chat in the tunnel, then get on the pitch and try to kick the shit out of each other. After the game, we'd shake hands, then meet in the Players' Lounge for a drink, and whatever had happened on the pitch would be forgotten. Until the next time.

Man United were different, however. First of all, they'd always come out of the dressing room second. It wouldn't have mattered if we'd waited an hour to come down the tunnel, they'd have made sure they were there after us, no matter what. And even though I played against Ryan Giggs very often, we'd never really talk. You'd speak to whoever you wanted to speak to. And it never really went off in the tunnel, like it did when United played Arsenal that time. I was too focused on the game ahead to start having a go at anyone in the tunnel. Plus, as captain, I had to lead the boys out so needed to be on my best behaviour.

It was an unbelievable honour for me to be made captain of West Ham by Lou Macari. Alvin Martin wasn't best pleased about it, seeing as Lou had taken the armband off him, but it meant a lot to me, especially when I found out I was the club's youngest skipper since Bobby Moore. No pressure then.

Seriously, I didn't feel any pressure being the captain because that team was full of senior professionals who were all like captains. Most of the time, it just felt like my only job was to flip the coin before kick-off.

I was as verbal as anyone else on the pitch, but I'd always encourage someone who might have been having a bad game, because that can happen to anyone.

If it all went off on the training pitch, any number of the lads would have stepped in to calm things down. Back then, it wasn't a case of the captain taking all the players' concerns to the manager. At that time, if a player had an issue or wanted something, they'd go and talk to the gaffer themselves.

There were always senior players I could talk to, so I never felt like there was any pressure on me at all. Now and again, you might let one of the apprentices have it as the captain, especially if they'd stepped out of line. In that respect, I had learned the hard way myself when I was at Birmingham, and it was those experiences which kept me so grounded, even when I became West Ham skipper at the age of 22.

Taking on the captaincy role seemed light years away from when I first started out in football as a teenager. When I was an apprentice at Birmingham, a senior player used to smash on the door of the changing room when he was getting changed, until an apprentice would emerge. I'd come along and he'd say something like 'get me a fucking towel!' In those days, the players took charge of everything, and had us apprentices working our bollocks off.

Not that the managers then weren't also capable of making sure our feet stayed firmly on the ground. When John Bond took over at Birmingham, I was still a kid with a lot to learn. I loved John because he was brilliant to work with, really funny, and knew so much about the game.

On his first morning in charge, John was taking training so he could have a look at what we were all about. I was playing in a front two alongside Wayne Clarke, and John was yelling out instructions from the sidelines for a drill that we were working on.

As the ball was played forward towards us, John shouted 'Julian, spin and go away, spin and go away!' but I had no idea what he meant.

We tried it again, and he yelled 'spin away, spin away!' but I still had absolutely no idea what I was supposed to do, and John wasn't showing me what he meant, instead just gesticulating dramatically with his hands.

We set it up a third time, with the same result and that was enough for John. 'Right, you fuck off over there and train with the kids!'

I certainly understood what he meant that time, and I had to walk off the pitch with my head practically between my legs, thinking 'fuck me, that was a good start.'

John was excellent at keeping everyone grounded, and his predecessor Ron Saunders was exactly the same. Even at the age of 16, I was on the fringes of the Birmingham first team, often training with the professionals, despite still being an apprentice.

One Saturday afternoon at St Andrew's, Ron called me into the dressing room with an air of urgency.

'You're playing,' he said.

'What?'

'Get in here, and get your kit on, you're starting the game. One of the lads has gone down with an illness. I need you.'

I couldn't believe what I was hearing as I went into the changing room and put the kit on as quickly as I could.

As I sat there, I was a bag of nerves. I thought I felt ready to play my first game of professional football, but my heart was beating fast, and my mouth had gone completely dry.

I looked around the room and saw all these men ready to give their all for Birmingham, and it put a seed of doubt in my mind, even though I was normally a cocky little sod.

I sat there for around 10 minutes, until Ron came back in and told me that he was joking. I wasn't playing after all. The truth is, although I was a bit gutted at his cruel prank, I was mightily relieved as well. It was all part of Ron's strategy to make sure I didn't get too big for my boots. He also wanted to give me a taste of sitting in the dressing room before a game so that when my time did come, it wouldn't be a completely new experience for me. There was definitely some method in his madness.

Even after I'd made my Birmingham debut at 17, and then became a regular starter at 18, I wasn't exactly living the life of a superstar footballer.

Before a match, I used to get the bus to the ground from where I was living which was a journey of around three miles. That was fine when I originally started playing for the first team, but it became a problem once people started to recognise me. And when I say people, I mean Aston Villa fans. They would get on the same bus and give me no end of grief about being a Bluenose, and that me and my club were both shit. As I would fully expect them to, given the city rivalry between our two clubs.

So I went to see the Birmingham chairman Ken Wheldon. Ken was a former scrap dealer, who was the same size as Danny DeVito, and was a lovely bloke. I told him about the abuse I was getting on the bus from the Villa fans.

'Fucking hit 'em!' was his somewhat unhelpful reply.

I explained that I couldn't really do that, but a sponsored car would help as my salary of £140 per week made it impossible for me to buy my own motor. He very kindly told me to leave it with him.

Shortly after that, one of the club sponsors managed to get me a car. It was an FSO, straight out of Poland, which was a bit like driving a square box on wheels. And it came with the bonus feature of 'Birmingham City Community' written down its side. I didn't care one bit. In fact, I loved it as it gave me a bit of freedom and spared me the Villa fans' abuse.

The biggest relief I had at that time, however, wasn't stopping getting on the bus to matches. It was actually the end of my apprenticeship, and therefore the end of all the incredibly hard work I had to do around the club and the training ground.

The youth team coach was a guy called Keith Bradley and he was very strict with us. As well as cleaning the senior players' boots, we also had to scrub the whole training ground to make sure it was in tip top shape for the following day. Worse than that, on Fridays we went over to St Andrew's, where we would clean the changing rooms, showers and toilets, then put all the match kit out, checking that the players' boots were spotless. We also had to walk around the stadium, picking up litter and putting it in the bins – those terraces were absolutely enormous so that was really hard work.

All that would mean that I never got home until 9 p.m. on a Friday, and you have to remember that as an apprentice I was only on £15 a week.

On top of that, once a week there would be The Blitz, where we had to make sure that everything was absolutely spotless. It wasn't a case of just cleaning the floors, we also had to make sure the skirting boards, lights and plug sockets were all as clean as a whistle. Keith would inspect our work by rubbing his finger along any surface, and if he found any dust then we had to do it all over again.

Once I started playing for the first team, even though I was only 17, I was no longer an apprentice which meant I didn't have to do all those chores that all the other 16-18-year-olds at the club were doing.

It was an absolute result for me, except nobody had bothered to tell Keith. One day, he came up to me and told me I had to clean one of the rooms at the training ground.

'No, I fucking don't,' was my reply.

'Yeah, you do. Now do it.'

'No, I don't have to anymore.'

And on it went until Martin Kuhl stepped in. I'd always got on well with Martin, who had kind of looked out for me, from when I first arrived at Birmingham, aged 14. We were now both in the first team, so Martin reminded Keith of that fact. 'Keith, Julian's a pro now so fuck off.' Job done. Or not done as it turned out.

But just because I never had to clean another room again didn't mean I forgot all about those experiences. Whether it was driving the FSO or getting the bus to games, those early days ensured that I would never take my football career for granted.

Likewise, when I became West Ham captain, I didn't let it go to my head. Being captain never affected the way I played either, despite some managers insisting that I had to lead by example, and yellow and red cards were not the way to do that. But that wasn't me at all. I would always be the same player whether I had the captain's armband on or not.

Despite picking up more than my fair share of cards, I actually got on quite well with some of the referees, who were nothing like some of the robots that have come into the game in more recent years.

I always had a good rapport with Roger Milford. I'm not sure if it was because we were both from Bristol, but we would always have a laugh and a joke together. One thing you could always guarantee with Roger was that his face would be suntanned, and his hair immaculate. He was a proper character.

I remember one game when I felt some of his decisions weren't quite as good as he looked, so I ran past him and said, 'You're having a fucking nightmare!'

'Don't swear at me,' he replied, 'you ain't seen your fucking game!'

It definitely put a smile on my face, although I'm not sure Bryan Robson was smiling when the pair clashed in a Man United game. After one typically tough Robson tackle too many, Roger had had enough, and he went to his pocket to produce the yellow card. As he was rummaging around, Bryan said something along the lines of 'Do you know who I am?' only for Roger to reply 'You're Bryan Robson, fuck off!' and book him.

Keith Hackett was another great character who you could share a joke with, without the risk of getting into trouble. Mind you, I always felt like I might get into hot water with Keith as he looked a bit like a headmaster. Just looking at him used to remind me of that scary feeling of seeing the head at school.

Back then, you could get away with talking back to the refs, or even swearing at them. They recognised that football was a passionate, working-class game, and that was all part of it. I'd often have a go at the ref, only to be told to fuck off.

Fair enough. In one reserve game I played in at Upton Park, I smashed into some kid and the ref gave a foul against me and said, 'You do that again, and I'll send you off.'

'Fuck off!' I replied.

'Swear at me again and I'll send you off.'

'Fuck off, course you won't.'

And so it went on between us. It was almost a part of the game then as some referees understood the language of football in a way that they don't today.

When I was coaching with Slaven Bilic at West Ham and West Brom, I'd have to go through the whole teamsheets thing with the referees, just like I did when I was Hammers captain all those years before.

And if I hated it as a player, I absolutely detested it as a coach. Every single referee would always say the same thing, as if they were reading from a script. It was as if the FA had created a tribe of robot refs, and almost made me feel sorry for today's players. I said almost.

•

I hear a huge roar from the fans as the final whistle goes.

That feels good. A job well done. It's time for more hand-shaking, as if there hasn't been enough of that today.

But this is different. The game's over, and it's time to acknowledge the other team as fellow professionals who have also given their all, but that just wasn't enough today.

I walk across to the nearest oppo player, grab his hand and say 'well played' and that begins a chorus of 'played' across the pitch.

I work my way around the team, then shake the ref's hand too – well, I am the captain after all.

Now, I go over to the fans and clap them too. I don't actually do a lap of the ground, as that would be over the top for winning three points.

I walk towards each stand and applaud, making it clear that I'm grateful for all the support, because I really am. As always, they were absolutely magnificent today, and right now I need them to know that.

As I'm clapping, I think about the fans and how they're just like me, living for the weekend. I'm glad and proud of the shift I put in for them today.

All around the stadium, I can hear the sound of clapping. I can also see the numbers inside the ground thinning as the supporters leave. Like me, they might be heading off for the pubs around Upton Park, or going home to their families.

I'm walking off the pitch, back towards the tunnel now, and there are loads of fans who are leaning out over the ad hoardings, some with pens in their hands.

I sign a few autographs. I always do. We chat while I sign. These are the people who are paying my wages. These are the people who I play for. I don't understand players who could ever walk past them. Plus, I love it. I really love it.

When the autographs are signed, I walk back down the two flights of stairs, past the away dressing room, and into our own changing room.

I walk into a great atmosphere. Immediately, I hear laughter, and the sound of happy chatter. Some of the lads are already in towels, having had their showers. Others are in various stages of undress. The dressing room is not a place for anyone with inhibitions.

There's a bit of chat about the game between the lads in the corner. Others are discussing plans for the evening, the pubs and clubs that will need to be visited.

I join in with my opinion on that crucial matter while I pull off my shirt. Whatever happens, we will all go to the Players' Lounge first, that's a given.

The noise dies down because the gaffer wants to say a few words. There's silence now, as we listen to him.

He finishes and there's a lot of noise – shouts, claps and general joy.

I head into the shower, and I'm already thinking about a well-earned pint.

After the shower, I put my pre-match suit back on. I like looking the part before and after the game, and I always take good care of my gear.

As I get dressed, I look around the room and see that it's already half-empty.

The kit man is picking up the scattered shirts, shorts and socks from all over the floor. The apprentices are gathering up boots like their lives depend on it. And they do.

The gaffer has gone to speak to the press, it's all part of his job. He's certainly going to look good today, as we all are.

I walk out of the dressing room, but this time I'm not heading down the tunnel to the pitch. I'm heading up to the Players' Lounge.

The door to the lounge is opened for me by a steward and I'm instantly hit by the smoke-filled atmosphere of the room. It's pretty busy with players from both teams, and plenty of family members in today as well.

Through the smoke and the people, I see the bar and I'm walking towards it to get my beer. I say a few hellos on the way, to the people I know, the mums, dads, wives, brothers and sisters of my team-mates. All familiar faces now that I've been at the club for a while.

All my hellos are returned with 'played' or 'well played' and now I'm at the bar, and I've got a beer in my hand. I raise it to some of those around me, and have a sip. It tastes good. The taste of victory.

I find my mum, and we have a chat. She's been watching me play since I was a kid, and she was always vocal on the sidelines. At Upton Park, it's hard to hear her but I'm sure she's cheering me on.

We have a catch up, and I talk to a few other people, but I feel restless. The adrenaline rush of the game is still with me. It takes a while to leave my system.

THE CAPTAIN

I head out of the lounge, and walk down to the gym, where some of us were pissing around with a ball much earlier today.

We were trying to kick a ball against the light switch, to see if we could turn it off from ten yards away.

Now, the gym is full of kids having a kickabout while their parents have a drink. I recognise a few of them as I see these faces every other week.

Now that I'm in here, it would be rude not to get involved, so I find a ball and start pinging it against the wall. Some of the kids join in with me, and suddenly we're having a little game, and I'm messing around and making them laugh.

It doesn't feel like I've been in here two minutes, and one of my team-mates pokes his head around the door, asking me if I'm coming for a drink.

It's time to finish in here. Two games of football is enough for one day. I put my jacket on, head back to the lounge to say a few goodbyes, and then seven or eight of us head out of the stadium.

It's probably more than an hour and a half since the game ended, but there are still fans waiting outside the players' entrance, as we walk out of there.

Someone thrusts a pen in my hand, and I start signing more autographs on scraps of paper. A few fans have photos that they want signed. They're photos of me which they probably bought in the club shop so I scribble my signature on them, and have a quick chat.

HAMMER TIME

As I sign each one, they drift off into the East End night. Now the last of them leaves, and so do I. I head off to catch up with my team-mates as it's also time for us to drift off into the night. Or the pub, as some people call it.

THE ENTERTAINERS

One Fat Boy, a ginger Welshman
and the kid the missus fancies

A cow and some sheep. And a load of fields. Those are pretty much the highlights of the journey so far. It ain't exactly exciting.

I yawn, as I stare out of the window, looking for something interesting but finding not very much at all.

I start to daydream about what fans must imagine these journeys to be like. They probably think it's an absolute riot in here, with music, banter and all sorts.

I can't say it's exactly like that right now. Maybe on the way back from a game that we've won it can get a bit lively, as we might all have a few drinks, but not right now.

I look around the bus. Towards the front, the gaffer, coaches, kit man and physio are all sitting, either talking quietly, or just doing fuck all. A bundle of laughs they are not.

I'm sitting in the middle, and a few players around me are watching a film on the coach TV, while Martin Allen is reading a book. I have no idea what the fuck that is all about, and I've already told him that.

Behind us are some curtains which divide the coach in

two. Behind them, there's a bit more noise as that's where some of the lads are playing cards, around a horseshoe-shaped seating area.

To be honest, it doesn't sound like they're having that much fun, as I think it's quite a high stakes game.

I don't get why they would play for so much money, but I suppose they must be as bored as I am right now.

Also behind the curtain is the toilet – I don't think I really need to explain that any further.

I'm looking forward to getting out of here, and into our hotel. Especially for my steak dinner, and then a few JD night-caps. I've got my traditional away trip bottle safely stashed away in my bag.

I don't get nervous before games, but I do get a fair amount of nervous energy as we get closer to a match, so sitting here trapped on this coach is not helping me deal with that.

Out of the window, yet more fields go past, but this time there are no animals in sight.

The motorway is fairly busy given that it's Friday, but it's not too bad and we haven't hit any horrible traffic yet. That would really do my head in.

I hear a laugh or two coming from my right, and look up at one of the lads watching the film. It sounds funny, but I can't get involved in a film on the coach. That just doesn't work for me.

I grab the sandwich which is on the seat next to me, and take a bite. There's always plenty of food on these journeys, but I don't like eating just for the sake of it. Because I'm bored. Yet, that's kind of what I'm doing right now.

'Yes!' I hear shouted from behind me, from the direction of the card game. Someone's just won big, but I can't tell whose voice it is.

Whoever it is has just become a tiny bit richer, but it doesn't sit right with me. If you're on the way to a game, why would you gamble so much money?

I mean having a few drinks on the night before a match is one thing, but losing £600 or £700 on the way there is pointless.

Instead of focusing on the game, that person will then be thinking about getting the money back on the way home. Their mind won't be right at all. I just don't get it.

It's winding me up right now, just thinking about it. I've never really been the type to gamble, it's just not my thing, but I understand people will enjoy it. But there's got to be a time and a place for it, right?

How can 24 hours before a match be the right time? It pisses me off.

I turn to look back out of the window. I see some sheep. And more fields. On the right, a car drives past the coach, and it's got kids frantically waving out of their windows. I think they're doing it to everyone, not just us because we're West Ham.

I'm bored. I can often get like this before a game but being stuck on the coach is really annoying me at the moment.

I get up out of my seat. I need the loo. At the very least, it's a change of scenery, and something to do. This is how bored I am.

I open the curtains in the middle of the coach. In front of me, there are six serious faces, staring at the cards in their hands. In the middle of the table is a deck of cards, and next to that is a big pile of fivers and tenners.

They don't even look up at me, or say a word. I look at each of them and they're all very focused on the game.

As I walk past the table, I grab all the cards from the middle of the table and start ripping them to pieces. I rip every last card and let them drop to the coach floor.

'What the fuck have you done that for?' I hear.

'Fucking arsehole,' I also hear, followed by 'wanker'.

I'm smiling. Grinning from ear to ear, and I carry on walking past the table and to the toilet where I go in and lock the door.

As I'm peeing, I can't get the smile off my face. That's the end of their game.

I come out of the loo, and I can see everyone on the coach is looking in my direction but I don't care.

I walk back to my seat, and stare out of the window. I see some more sheep but this time, I'm smiling.

•

Maybe I was a bit of a sod at times, but I like to think I was making a point. It never made any sense to me that people

were gambling huge sums of money right before an important game. To this day, I have no idea why the managers
would allow it, as it so clearly could have made an impact
on someone's mental state so close to a match.

And I did the card-ripping act more than once. I found it
quite funny, because they were so wrapped up in their card
game, they'd barely notice I was there. It was very easy work.
Admittedly, I was also acting out of boredom and not just on
a principle. But sometimes I'd do daft pranks on those coach
journeys as well.

I could never understand Martin Allen's love of reading
books, I just thought it was weird. At that time, you just
didn't seen many footballers reading so it confused me. On
one journey, he nipped to the loo and left his book in his
seat, so I went over there and ripped out a load of pages,
tearing them into tiny pieces like confetti. I thought that was
hilarious, although poor Martin definitely disagreed.

Despite winding him up at times, I loved Martin and I
think his passion for the game matched mine. I remember
he used to run his own soccer school during the school
holidays, where hundreds of children would turn up for
a week's worth of football coaching. Not only did Martin
provide the kids with a full day of football, he also made
sure that three West Ham players would be there as well
to make it even more special for the young hopefuls. And
as the camp was held in Basildon in Essex, this was serious

West Ham territory, so the kids would get to meet, or even be coached by, some of their heroes.

I absolutely loved it when Martin asked me to help him out at his camps – I think I was probably more excited than the kids as the camps took place at the end of May when our season was over and I was missing training, and just generally playing football.

Martin told me to get there at 9.30 a.m., so I made sure I turned up a full hour earlier in order that I could help with getting the camp set up. Just after 8.30 a.m., I was carrying a five-a-side goal across the pitch, much to Martin's dismay, who told me I didn't need to do that as he had other staff who could do that. I just ignored him.

Shortly after, I bumped into Martin as I was carrying three big bags full of size five footballs, which were pretty heavy to be fair. Again, he said I didn't have to do that, and again, I paid no attention to what he was saying. What Martin didn't understand was that I wasn't the kind of person who would turn up to a soccer school as one of three professional players, and just strut around as if I owned the place and not get my hands dirty. Whatever I do, I do it properly, and this was no exception.

That's why when lunchtime came around and everyone sat around eating sandwiches and having a cup of tea, I'd still be out there playing football with the kids, and having fun. If I ever got hungry, I'd just ask the kids for a sandwich or something, because there was no way I would ever have brought my own lunch with me.

The whole thing was a huge bonus for me as it meant I got to play football every day for a week, at a time when I would otherwise have been sitting around at home. And hopefully, the way I approached his camps, meant Martin forgave me for ripping up his book.

Doing stupid things like that was par for the course for me back then. I used to let tyres down in the training ground car park, and stick washing-up liquid in everyone's drink bottles. And if I hadn't let someone's tyres down, they wouldn't be able to get into their car anyway because I'd nicked their car keys. Stuff like that was always going on throughout my time in football, with everyone getting involved, although sometimes we'd be a little bit more sophisticated and elaborate with the pranks.

We once told Stuart Slater that Lee Clayton from the *Sun* was coming to Chadwell Heath to interview him, and that he had to make a really good impression in order to come across well in the paper. We told him that we all usually wore suits for these kind of press interviews, with a three-piece suit being the best look he could possibly go for. I'm pretty sure that Stuart went out and bought himself a new three-piece suit for the interview, which obviously never took place. And there were others who also fell for that one.

The pranks on the coach were certainly born out of bore-dom, meaning the way back from a game would have a very different feel about it. If we'd won the match, those journeys formed some of the best memories of my career. We were never drunk on the way home, but we'd always have a few celebratory drinks, before carrying on once we had returned home. And even though there was a strong drinking culture back then, everyone would be included in a celebration on the way home, whether they were drinkers or not.

On the way home, the horseshoe seats would be a different kind of space, far more sociable, and we would all be together. We won as a team and celebrated as a team.

By then, things had already changed enormously, because we were staying overnight, meaning the coach journey there was the day before the return trip. That might sound obvious, but there were plenty of games while I was playing at Birmingham, and early on at West Ham, when we would have travelled there and back on the same day. I can distinctly remember doing that when we played at Aston Villa.

With money tight at Birmingham, that was often the only option when I first started playing, but thankfully that changed as my career progressed. As more money started to come into the game, not only were we able to enjoy the relative luxury of travelling up to matches the night before and staying in hotels, but we were also able to treat ourselves to presents that I could never have imagined when I was cleaning out the toilets and showers at Birmingham's training ground.

A good example of that is when I bought myself a Harley-Davidson Fat Boy for £13,000, which was a fair whack back in the early nineties. And when you consider that I didn't have a licence to ride the bike, and that therefore I also wasn't insured on it, it was a bit of an extravagance, to say the least.

But I loved it. It was such good fun, and it looked and sounded incredible. I had the slashed exhaust pipes so that thing was fucking loud, you could hear me coming from miles away. Sitting on it, I couldn't even hear myself think. What a buzz.

I started riding it into the training ground, which was probably a mistake, but there was no point in owning it and just letting it sit at home. As always, Charlie was on the gate at Chadwell Heath waving me in, but for some reason Billy Bonds didn't hear the bike, even though you could probably have heard it at Upton Park.

On my way out of training that day, I probably revved that Fat Boy a little too hard as I left, and shot up the road. Apparently, Billy came out of his office and asked Charlie what the noise was.

'It's Julian,' said Charlie.

'What, on a fucking motorbike?' said the gaffer.

'Yeah,' confirmed Charlie, a reliable witness as ever.

Inevitably, the next day at training, Billy pulled me into his office, to explain that I couldn't ride the bike. He told me it was in my contract that it wasn't allowed.

I was enjoying myself far too much on that bike so I said ok, and carried on riding it into training anyway.

My plan was to park it down the road from the training ground on Saville Road, and see if I could get away with it. But those crazy loud slash pipes meant that it was too hard for me to go incognito on the bike, and Billy heard it again.

'Look,' he said. 'You can't ride that bike. If you come off it, your insurance won't cover you because you're a footballer.'

'Billy,' I replied. 'I don't have insurance because I'm a footballer, they won't cover me. And I don't have a licence either because I can't be bothered doing the lessons.'

Billy looked at me, and I thought his eyes were going to pop right out of his head.

'Are you fucking mad?' he said. 'No more!'

And that was it for the Fat Boy. I had to sell it at a loss, and not just a financial hit. I missed riding it, and I really missed just looking at it, marvelling at the beauty of that machine.

But that wasn't it for me and motorbikes as a West Ham player. In fact, it was thanks to a motorbike that I was even able to play one particular game for the Hammers, as I had a problem with my car.

At that time, unlike today when players stay together in a hotel overnight even before a home fixture, we'd have to make our own way to Upton Park on a matchday. One Saturday, I left my house at around 11.30 a.m. as usual and was cruising down the A127 looking forward to the match as always. Unfortunately, at that point my car decided it wasn't looking forward to the game as much as I was, and conked out on me.

There was no getting it going again, so I had to leave it in a lay-by, and then I desperately started flagging down passing cars, as I couldn't risk being late for the game. Eventually, a bloke on a motorbike pulled over so I told him the situation, which I neatly summed up as 'I'm Julian Dicks, and I need to get to Upton Park.'

He invited me to jump on the bike behind him, but he didn't have a spare crash helmet for me, so I had to take a bit of a risk. We bombed it the rest of the way down the A127, then on to Upton Park where I hopped off the bike, ran into the stadium and made sure my saviour was given a ticket for the game. It was the least I could do as I would never have made it there on time without him.

Whether that man's bike or my own Harley, they were certainly a step up from any other mode of transport I'd previously experienced. I'd already come a long way from the FSO at Birmingham, and the Fiesta I was so thrilled to own when I first arrived at West Ham.

Times were changing and as even more money came into the game, our car options improved, as did the size of the squad, as new signings would arrive at Chadwell Heath with increasing frequency. Especially when Harry Redknapp was in charge.

The amount of players that came through those training

ground gates in those times was unbelievable. It felt like it never ended. We'd be training and Harry would gather us round with a really excited look in his eyes. 'You won't believe who I've got coming in next week,' he'd say, as if he was a schoolkid collecting football stickers.

On that occasion, he was referring to Romanian star Ilie Dumitrescu, but it could have been Paulo Futre, Florin Raducioiu, or Dani, the good-looking Portuguese kid about whom Harry memorably remarked: 'My missus fancies him. Even I don't know whether to play him or fuck him!'

You had to laugh when Harry paired Dani up front with veteran striker Iain Dowie, an absolutely top bloke, but not someone who was especially known for his looks. It was a bit like having beauty and the beast up top.

Harry may have been fond of a signing or two, but to be fair to him, he was an incredibly successful manager for the Hammers. Under Harry, we finished in our highest Premier League position so he was obviously doing something right. As a former Hammer himself, he knew exactly what the fans wanted, and expected everyone to give everything they had on the pitch, but to also play football the West Ham way. That was really important to him, and to all of us.

There were still contrasting styles of football at that time, with Wimbledon enjoying a lot of success with their more direct approach. With all the money coming into the game, it would have been tempting to ditch the passing game, and chase the prizes at any cost. But, to his credit, Harry stuck to the principles he'd been raised on at West Ham, and still enjoyed a great deal of success. There may have been a few questionable signings here and there, but he made some superb moves in the market as well.

I remember when he brought in John Hartson and Paul Kitson, two quality strikers, both of whom scored loads of important goals for the club that helped keep us in the Premier League, including in that famous 4–3 win against Spurs.

John was a big, red, ginger Welsh thug, and I don't say that because of the Eyal Berkovic incident. I played against him when he was at Arsenal, and he was as strong as an ox, a really fiery, aggressive striker who was so hard to play against. And he was a really good footballer too, make no mistake about that. He slotted in very well at West Ham, and I can still picture him sitting at the back of the coach with a beer in his hand after an away game. In many ways, John was an old school centre-forward, one of the last of a dying breed.

You could also have a laugh and a joke with Harry, and he would have a drink with us too – he didn't hit the Essex clubs with us as that would have been a step too far, but he'd often be up for a drink and a chat. That's not to say he didn't have another side to him, and I'm sure I won't be the first or last to say that about Harry. He could let you have it if it was required, as Don Hutchison found out when the plate of salmon sandwiches flew past his head at Southampton.

There was another game we'd lost when Harry came into the dressing room, and he was clearly unhappy. Ilie Dumitrescu was a very exciting player for us, who'd run at the opposition with the ball, and get bums off seats in the stands. But, on this particular day, Harry was unhappy and picked out a few players for criticism, including Ilie.

I could see that Ilie was not best pleased with being spoken to like that by Harry, so he picked up his boot and threw it towards the gaffer. I don't think it actually hit the gaffer, but suddenly Harry squared right up to Ilie, and the pair were eyeball to eyeball.

Harry was livid, and Ilie was not holding back either. The remarkable thing was that nobody stood in between them in an attempt to defuse the situation. I actually remember thinking how funny it would be if Ilie and Harry actually came to blows, and was fully prepared to see if it went that far.

After a long stand-off between the pair, Harry's assistant Frank Lampard jumped in between them, and calmed it all down, which was probably a sensible way to resolve the situation, but also slightly disappointing from where I was sitting.

Clearly, I had the odd run-in with Harry, but overall he was pretty good to me. That was especially the case after a naughty night out I had with Kenny Brown and Don Hutchison, shortly after I arrived back at West Ham from Liverpool.

It was a Thursday, and everyone knew that you don't go out on a Thursday or Friday night before a Saturday game. It wasn't even up for debate, it was just part of the rules. We would go out on any other night of the week, not necessarily in the same week although sometimes we did, but Thursdays and Fridays were sacred.

And Kenny, Don and myself had no intention of going out on that particular Thursday. We'd all been at training together, and decided to reward our hard work with a trip into Romford to get some lunch.

I'm sure plenty of people can relate to leaving work for a spot of lunch, having a drink or two, then sacking off the rest of the day, and really going for it. Well, that's exactly what we did. We had a couple of drinks with our lunch, but probably enjoyed them a bit too much. It got to what you might call make or break time, the moment when your brain has to make a sensible decision, one that isn't fuelled by alcohol, even though there's a bit of alcohol in your system.

Turns out that was a challenge we failed, as we unanimously thought 'fuck it' and decided to stay out drinking in the pubs and bars of Romford. It was probably not the smartest move, not just because it was a Thursday and we weren't allowed to do that, but also because Romford wasn't exactly under the radar. It was very much West Ham territory, and just a stone's throw from the training ground. But we certainly were not thinking about that at the time. I'm pretty sure we weren't thinking at all, but we were definitely having a lot of fun.

Eventually, I got back to Kenny's place at 3 a.m., making it one of the longest lunches on record. The following morning I woke up at 9.50 a.m. which wasn't ideal given that we had to be at the training ground at 10 a.m. I called the training ground and asked to speak to Harry.

'Harry, someone's broken into my car,' I said. 'I'll be a bit late as I need to sort it out.'

'No problem, Julian,' said the gaffer.

Job done. Well, sort of. We still had to get into the training ground and sweat the alcohol out of our system, which was not going to be an easy job. It was a bit like *Mission Impossible*, but we had to give it our best shot.

I was probably still a bit pissed from the night before, but I drove down to Chadwell Heath anyway, definitely not feeling great. Once we got there, I went to see Shirley who worked in the canteen as I knew she'd be on-board with whatever we needed. She gave us a load of bin bags, which we put on under our training gear, then went out to train, and sweated our bollocks off.

We then showered off, had some lunch at the training ground, and then it was back home for some well-earned sleep. We'd pulled off a great heist.

This was the days before every club had a sports science department, but we were well ahead of the curve on that one. Admittedly, they wouldn't have recommended drinking on a Thursday night before a Saturday game, but they would have been proud of our efforts to combat the effects of the alcohol.

Come Saturday, it was Leicester at home, and it all went wrong for Don as he was sent off. Fortunately for him, and for myself as it turned out, I scored a penalty and we won 1–0, completing a great 48 hours.

We had a day off on the Sunday, and then it was back to the training ground on Monday, but I realised something was up when Harry called Hutch and me into his office to see him. I knew that he wouldn't do that just for a red card.

I waited outside while Hutch went in to face the music.

He told me after that he went in there, sat down, and Harry said to him, 'You were out on Thursday, weren't you? Tell me the truth or I'm going to fine you as much as I possibly can.'

And Hutch folded like one of the bad card players at the back of the coach. Harry fined him two weeks' wages for the red card, and two weeks for going out on a Thursday – I'd have been interested to know what he was planning on fining him if he *hadn't* admitted what he'd done!

I went in to see Harry, and he said to me, 'You were out on Thursday, weren't you?'

'Yeah, gaffer, I was but I promise you that it won't happen again,' I said.

'Ok, no problem,' said Harry, and that was it. He let me off the hook.

When Hutch heard that I'd been let off, he went crazy. He wanted to go back in to see Harry to complain that I hadn't been fined. I had to tell him to sit down, shut up, and not to be so stupid. I did feel bad for him though – he was missing out on a month's wages for a long lunch and a red card, which seemed a tad harsh to say the least.

But that was Harry. He could be very tough, but he could also be your best mate. If I'm honest, I thought he was probably going to throw the book at me for going out on a Thursday, and he would have had every right to do so. Somehow, potentially because of my performance against Leicester, he let me get away with it. I'd not been back from Liverpool for long, so it's possible he wanted to ease me back in to West Ham, and might have foreseen me reacting badly to a punishment at that stage. So maybe it was some inspired Harry man management.

Hutch, however, was fairly new at the club and maybe Harry wanted to show him that he wasn't a pushover, and make sure that Don knew he couldn't cross certain lines.

Don turned out to be a great player for West Ham, one of many that Harry signed for the club. As well as Kitson and Hartson, Ian Wright joined the club towards the end of my career. Obviously, Wrighty was a class player and an incredible goalscorer, but he was also the most magnificent bloke off the pitch as well. He was a genuinely lovely man, and it was a joy to play football with him.

I'd never had a team-mate who was so full of life. He was

permanently buzzing around, and had boundless energy. It's an over-used phrase, but there really would never be a dull moment with Ian around.

Mind you, at times his lively, happy nature was the last thing I needed, especially if some of us had been out the night before. I might be feeling a bit worse for wear, and Wrighty would be his usual loud, cheerful self and then I'd have to say 'Wrighty, leave me alone!' I think he probably quite enjoyed those moments too.

At that time, the dressing room was also home to three young players who had come through the club's famed academy, and blossomed into incredible talents, and who were a massive asset to West Ham.

I was in my late 20s at the time, unfortunately very close to having my career ended early by injury, and I was well aware of a changing-of-the-guard type of feeling with the emergence of Joe Cole, Rio Ferdinand and Frank Lampard, or 'Little Frank' as we called him to make sure that everyone knew we weren't talking about his dad, who was Harry's assistant.

I was never more aware of that than the day I came up against Joe in a one-on-one game on the training ground. I loved those situations, just the two of us and a ball, a battle of wits, skill and physical ability. But I didn't love Joe taking the piss.

He was an unbelievably talented player, who had the quickest feet you could ever imagine. He could turn you inside out in the blink of an eye with his trickery. And that's what he did to me that day.

I obviously prided myself on coming out on top of those battles in training. I was certainly not used to losing, and I never took that well.

So there we were on the training pitch. Joe Cole and Julian Dicks. The young talented upstart against a bit of a grizzly senior pro and club captain. Watching on from the sidelines were the rest of the Hammers squad, as well as Harry, and the coaches. At those moments, reputations were always on the line. Or so it felt to me anyway, because I played to win everything I did.

Joe had the ball and ran towards me, feigning to move this way and that, somehow taking the ball with him, as he darted all over the place. I kept my eye on the ball, and tried to ignore him.

As he came close to me, he moved to go right, then went left, and suddenly he was gone. He was past me, and somehow the ball had gone through my legs, and he'd picked it up behind me. I barely even moved. The little fucker had nutmegged me, and made me look a total fool.

My hands were on my head, and I was smiling, but it was an angry smile of frustration.

'Fucking hell, Joe, that was lovely!' called Harry. 'He's mugged you off there, Julian. Made you look absolute shit!'

As you can imagine, Harry's goading didn't exactly help me at that moment. I was absolutely fuming, as the banter rained down on me from the sidelines. At that moment, I strongly felt that Joe shouldn't have done that. It seemed disrespectful to me, given our positions at the club. In simple terms, he was taking the piss and there was no way I was going to put up with that.

Sometimes, the training ground can be a brutal place – well, it certainly was the way I trained. But, it could also be somewhere where there was a pecking order, and you had to defend yourself, and your status in a way. It was a bit primitive in that way, but that's how it was. I felt like I'd been challenged, and I had to respond.

We went at it again. It was the same scenario, as Joe started with the ball, except this time I had the bit between my teeth, and there was no scenario in my mind where he was going to get past me.

He started moving towards me with the ball, again giving it all the cocky, flashy movements, this way and that. As he approached me, I didn't even bother watching the ball, I just kept my eye on Joe, because I was only interested in taking him down. I didn't give a shit about the ball.

He was about two yards away from me, trying to turn past me, so I launched myself into a full-blooded, totally committed challenge, which took him clean out. I smashed him into next week.

He lay on the pitch in a crumpled heap, but unfortunately that was the way it had to be for me to reassert my authority. Fortunately, he wasn't hurt, and I apologised to him later.

Harry, meanwhile, was livid. 'What did you do that for?' he yelled at me.

'Because idiots like you wind me up!' I replied.

Don't get me wrong, Joe was a blinding player, absolutely superb and a real entertainer. I wasn't surprised to see him go on to do so well with Chelsea and England but I'm not sure he quite fulfilled the incredible talent and gift that he had.

Rio Ferdinand was someone who definitely managed to fulfil his potential. Even back then, it was obvious what a phenomenal talent he was, with so much ability. He was a defender who was so comfortable on the ball, it was almost frightening. At times in the early days, it could get him into trouble as he might hold on to the ball too long, or misplace a pass. He definitely had a mistake in him, but he was just starting his career and that was completely normal. His confidence was incredible as well. He was very young when he broke into the first team, just 17, but he held his own in the dressing room and, more importantly, on the pitch.

And then there was my boot boy, otherwise known as Little Frank. As an apprentice, he drew the short straw, as he had to clean my boots, and I was pretty demanding when it came to their cleanliness. I'm sure that's not surprising after the schooling I was given at Birmingham. It made me have high expectations when it came to stuff like that, and poor Frank got it in the neck as a result.

I once made him a special offer where I promised him a £100 bonus if he cleaned my boots properly for two months. Having cleaned a lot of boots myself back in my apprentice days, I knew how hard that was. There were days when you were just not going to care as much, and your effort would slip, so my incentive was to try to get Frank to maintain the high standards I wanted.

For the first few days, he did a marvellous job. The boots had never looked better, almost like I'd just taken them out of the box, and I was very happy. But then, predictably, I'd come into the dressing room, and they'd still have bits of mud on them, and were nowhere near the state that I expected them to be in. It was time to find Little Frank.

When I saw him, I chucked one of the boots right at him, and hit him with it. 'These are shit,' I said. 'There's no bonus for you now, but you make sure you keep cleaning them properly. If they're not spotless, I'll throw them at you again, and kick the fuck out of you on the training pitch!'

I'd suddenly turned into one of those senior pros whose boots I used to clean. What goes around, comes around. Football's funny like that.

To be fair to Little Frank, he took it all in good spirits, and never got pissed off. He was a cocky sod, perhaps because his dad and uncle were running the club, although

I'm not sure it helped him having those two watching his every move.

Apart from being a cracking player, he was also very resilient, a great quality to have as a footballer. I felt there were times when he wasn't playing well and probably should have been dropped, but it never happened. Yet, despite those dips in form, he would always bounce back from that.

He was also a tremendously hard worker. He trained his nuts off. Every single day, he was probably one of the first players to arrive at Chadwell Heath, and always the last out. He'd be practising his free-kicks, and working on his game as much as he could, way beyond what was expected.

As much as I loved West Ham and wanted the club to do well, I actually felt that Frank needed to get away from the club to develop. I'm sure there were plenty of Hammers fans who weren't happy about his move to Chelsea, but I was delighted for him, especially seeing how well he went on to perform for his new club and England. I can't say it came as a shock to me at all, as his quality was obvious from the first time he broke into the West Ham team.

•

By the time, Frank, Rio and Joe were regulars at the training ground and then in the first team, my days as a professional footballer were numbered. In fact, I wasn't sure if I was ever going to play again, when the same knee gave way again in 1997.

Having been through all the pain and bad decisions that were made the first time around, I was at least a bit more prepared for what to expect this time. But what I wasn't prepared for was West Ham's insulting offer to pay me off, rather than deal with the injury. The club offered to pay me off with six months' worth of money, despite me having three years left on my contract. I couldn't believe it. I'd given everything I possibly could for the club, risking wrecking my knee for life, and this was how they were offering to thank me for my efforts.

My surgeon John King suggested I see a US surgeon called Jim Cannon who was based in Alabama. He operated on American footballers who all had serious knee problems from the battering they took playing their sport, so he would be best placed to advise me on what I could do.

The club reluctantly agreed to allow me to go to the States to see Jim, buying two economy class tickets for myself and John Green. I asked if I could fly business given the discomfort I was feeling in my knee, but I was told that would have to be at my own expense. So, John and I took our economy seats and I numbed any potential pain by getting pissed with him on the journey across the Atlantic. That was courtesy of the airline, not West Ham, just for the record.

Jim was very honest with me when he had a look at my knee, and it wasn't good news. He thought I had a one in ten chance of the surgery being successful and allowing me to play again – I'd heard those odds before. He was also clear that there was a risk of me ending up having to walk with a stick, due to the long-lasting damage that I was potentially doing to my knee.

Even if there was only a 10 per cent chance of playing again, I felt it had to be worth it, so that I could at least give myself the opportunity. I wasn't prepared to give up on my career that easily.

I returned home with at least some hope that it wasn't all over for me. After a fair bit of wrangling, the club agreed to let me have the operation. There wasn't much choice anyway, as I was never going to accept their offer of six months, so if they wanted to get any value out of my three-year contract, it was in their interest to try to get me playing again.

The other thing that annoyed me is that they were insured for exactly this kind of career-threatening or career-ending injury. There was no need for them to play hard ball with me. It wasn't like I was some young player who had just joined the club. I was the club captain, and a loyal servant to West Ham for many years. It made no sense to me, and really pissed me off.

John King did the surgery again, and then it was back on the rehab route with John Green. Even though we were a few years down the line since the first surgery and recovery, there hadn't been any major medical breakthroughs in the area, and I was still facing an enormous lay-off.

Like I said, knowing what to expect definitely helped me in fighting my way back which was lucky because I was out for 18 months, missing the entire 1997/98 season in the process.

After loads more graft, golf and grit, I was able to resume training but I was only able to join the rest of the lads every other day, as I had to give my knee time to recover after each session. Every time I exercised my knee, it would swell up, showing me how much I probably wasn't doing myself any favours. Despite that, I managed to get myself to the point where I was ready to play, except my game had to change as a result of my knee.

Tackling was absolutely fine, but there was no way I could be consistently getting up and down the pitch, making overlapping runs anymore, so I had to simplify the way I played. But Harry had other ideas, which is why I knew the game was up for me when he played me as a wing-back in that game at Charlton. To make matters worse, I remember Danny Mills giving it large about how he'd battered me in that game – there was no way I could put up with that every week.

I knew that it was impossible for me to be effective in that position as it required me to do exactly what I was now incapable of doing. I think Harry also knew that, and that's why I got to the point where I could read the writing that was on the wall.

There was a bit of a stand-off again. I knew the club no longer wanted me, but I still had a contract and I insisted that they pay me up. It wasn't a great way to end my career, but eventually common sense prevailed, and West Ham paid up the contract and gave me a testimonial. At 29 years old, it was over. I was beyond gutted, but I knew then what I still know now. I loved every second of it, because I gave everything I possibly could to every minute I played. Including one of my knees.

•

I'm staring through the window at a field full of cows again. I'm far from home and far from happy.

The coach is silent. I can only hear the noise of the passing traffic, and the hum of the coach's engine.

I look around and see everyone staring into space, a bit like I'm doing. It's been exactly like this since we left Coventry. Nobody has said a word.

Some of the lads are sat around the horseshoe near the back, but they're not playing cards. Not because I ripped them up. That was another journey, another game, in another season.

They're all just sitting there, lost in thought, or maybe in a daze.

I don't know how long it will be until we make it back to the training ground, but it can't come soon enough. I just want to get home and drown my sorrows. And I'm probably not the only one.

The gaffer's at the front with the coaches, and I wonder how the poor sod is feeling. The buck stops with him which is a bit unfair really. He's not the only one to blame.

When a team gets relegated, which is exactly what has happened to us today, there are a combination of reasons why it happens. I've been thinking about it for a while, because relegations don't just happen. Yes, it's been confirmed today, but this is obviously the result of a whole season's worth of problems.

We weren't the best team in the league, that much is obvious, but I can't work out if we're really the worst. I'm not sure we are but I know there have been times when we haven't been good enough, when maybe certain players have let themselves down and not quite given as much as they could have.

I'm not being cocky when I say that I don't feel I'm included in that category. I know that I've given everything I possibly could have done in every game I've played this season. My game was in order.

Yes, I had a bit of bad luck here and there, as did the whole team. There's nothing you can do about that over a season, but I can look at myself in the mirror and know that I always gave 100 per cent.

I felt that this was the case before today, and I still feel it now. As I think this, a couple of cars with West Ham fans in them pass us. I can see the claret and blue scarves still flying proudly in the back windows of the cars.

I feel bad for them. The poor bastards have travelled across the country to watch us today, knowing what would happen if we lost. They still made the journey and spent their hard-earned money on petrol and match tickets.

And now they're on the same journey back home as us, thinking about what's happened. Just like I am. I wonder if there's any noise in their cars. If they're listening to music, or just talking to each other. Or if they're listening to the sound of silence like I am.

I walked across the pitch at the end of the match, when the ref's whistle confirmed our worst fears. We lost 1–0, meaning there was no way back for us. We were out of the top flight.

I looked around the pitch as my team-mates' heads went down, and the life seemed to drain out of them. There was nothing any of us could say, so I went over to the fans, no doubt including those people in the cars next to us, and applauded them for all their efforts.

I stood there for a while. Nobody else joined me which I wasn't happy about, but I also understood how gutted everyone was. They wanted to get out of there as much as I did.

But the fans meant too much to me, not to go and be there with them.

Their cars have disappeared off into the distance now, and I'm back to looking at the other traffic, and the endless fields.

There's some food knocking around, and some of the lads are eating, but I had a bit in the dressing room, and I really don't feel like eating at the moment.

Thinking about that reminds me of walking back into that dressing room an hour or two ago. What a horrible feeling that was. One that I never want to repeat.

I got in there after clapping the fans, and it was like walking into a morgue. You could have heard a pin drop. There was no banter, no plans being discussed for a night out, no post-match words from the gaffer.

I went into the shower, and even that was quiet save for the noise of the water hitting the floor, as I washed the sweat and mud off my body. The sweat that was now in vain.

Back in the changing room, we'd all got dressed in silence. It was as silent as this coach right now, but without even traffic or engine noises. Occasionally, we could hear a few shouts from the Coventry dressing room, but otherwise nothing.

We had then left the ground and boarded the coach in exactly the same way. There was nothing to be said.

This is one of the worst feelings that I've had in football and, sadly, it isn't the only relegation I've known. At least I have that experience to draw on.

I know that I will feel as gutted as I do now for a few days. I know that when I wake up tomorrow morning I will almost immediately feel a horrible reminder of what happened today, when I remember.

But I also know that the feeling won't last. In a few days, we'll regroup and set targets for the following season. We can come back from this. I know from experience. But it's too soon for any of that now.

Right now, I just have to continue staring out of the window with everyone else on the coach, thinking about being at home. I focus on that comforting thought of pouring myself some wine, or maybe a Jack Daniel's if there's any left in the bottle from last night.

Tonight is definitely a night to get pissed and try to forget about what's happened today.

The coach drives past some sheep in a field again, and I can't get home soon enough.

PART THREE

PART THREE

THE BOLEYN

They fly so high. They reach the sky

It feels exactly the same, but it's also completely different. I look around the dressing room and it's impossible to stop the memories from flooding in.

Suddenly, I'm surrounded by McAvennie, Slater, Potts, Bishop, Morley, Bonds, Martin, Devonshire and Miklosko.

And there's Rob Jenkins handing round the medicine bottle. I can almost smell it.

I look again and of course none of those faces are here. In fact, the dressing room has been given a serious makeover since I was last in here about 15 years ago.

I look around to where the washrooms used to be, and there's no sign of the bath where I'd sit before a game, happily tucking into my Coke and Mars.

So many changes, yet this all feels so familiar. It's hard to believe I'm back here again. I honestly didn't think this would ever happen, and of course, it's not as if I'm about to pull on a claret and blue shirt again.

But this might just be the next best thing.

I can hear the atmosphere building out in the stadium, just like it used to at this time. Not long to go now. The boys are in from their warm-up, and they've got their shirts on. They're ready.

The stereo is blasting out some right old shit. It's a far cry from the Guns N' Roses that Slav and I used to listen to in our hotel room as team-mates.

But it seems to work for the lads. They're pumped up, chomping at the bit. Some of them are bouncing up and down, others are sitting quietly. Same characters, different era.

The dressing room door opens and Slav walks in. He's wearing a smart shirt and trousers as if he's ready for a night out. I'm standing here in my West Ham tracksuit, and he's making me look like I'm ready for bed.

The stereo is silenced, as are the lads, who all sit down and listen to Slav.

It's the first home Premier League game of the season, and we won at Arsenal last week. There really isn't that much to say as confidence is high, so Slav keeps it brief.

When he finishes, there's lots of clapping and a few shouts from the lads. I'm standing towards the back of the room, looking on.

The lucky bastards. What I would give for one more chance to play at Upton Park, to go out there, and to give everything for the fans again.

My thoughts are interrupted by the buzzer. Probably just as well. A few more shouts from some of the players who need to do that.

Apparently, they don't head-butt dressing room doors anymore, or block tackle the walls in the gym. But they still shout a bit.

One by one, they walk out of the room and head down the tunnel, beginning the journey that ends on the pitch. I neither lead them out, nor go with them, instead staying back in the dressing room.

The kit man sorts out some of the gear that's been left all over the place, tidying the room up a bit and getting it ready for half time. He's got 11 brand new shirts with him for the second half. I still can't believe that.

I get out of his way and begin to make my own way down the tunnel with some of the other members of the coaching team. Again, it's the same as it used to be while also being so different.

I'm looking at all the memories on the walls as we walk down the tunnel and I'm suddenly interrupted by an enormous roar. The players are out.

I'm going up the stairs myself now, as calmly as I ever did, but I can't help feeling excited. It's amazing to be back here.

I hear 'Bubbles' and now, as I walk on the huge club crest at the pitchside, I see bubbles too. Loads of them being churned out of a bubble machine as the crowd roar 'Fortune's always hiding . . .'

It's difficult not to join in with them, but not as difficult as it is for me to not go straight out on to the pitch, like I always did.

I stop alongside the grass and look across the stadium to all the fans in each stand. What a place this is. It's so good to be back.

I turn around and walk to the dugout. It's the same place John Lyall, Lou Macari, Billy Bonds and Harry Redknapp all sat, but it's been touched up a bit.

The seats are fancier now, there's a bit more room in it which is just as well because there are quite a few of us to fit in here.

I go to take my seat and hear some of the fans calling my name. It warms my heart, and I break out into a smile and give them a wave. They all cheer. It's so good to be back here.

I sit down and look out on to the pitch as the players get ready for kick-off. It's weird to think that is a view I've so rarely seen. I was never a substitute. If I was fit, I played. And I can't remember being subbed too often either. I can certainly remember leaving the pitch early, but that was for other reasons.

So here I am. Julian Dicks, West Ham coach. Sitting in the dugout. What an amazing feeling this is. It's not a patch on playing, but it's not too bad.

The bottom line is that I'm back at Upton Park, and I just love this place so much. The referee blows his whistle. Come on you Irons!

•

We lost that game. Leicester at home. It sounds like a bad result for our first home match of the season, especially after winning at Arsenal the week before. But when you remember that Leicester ended up winning the league that season, it is put into a bit of context.

It was a glorious season, as Slav did a superb job, but there was always a sadness in the background as we knew it was the club's last year at Upton Park. That place meant so much to me that it was kind of fitting that I was able to return there for a season-long farewell. In a way, I had to be there.

Call it fate, call it whatever you like, but somehow the stars aligned when I got a phone call from Slav's agent in June 2015 telling me that he wanted me to be his coach at West Ham. We all met up in a hotel in London, and it was great to see my old team-mate again. I didn't need any convincing at all, and in terms of qualifications I already had my B coaching licence and was working on adding an A licence to that.

Nearly 20 years before, Slav and I had been room-mates. We'd drink wine and smoke cigarettes while listening to the likes of Iron Maiden, AC/DC, Guns N' Roses and Metallica in our hotel room on the night before a game. That was if one of us had remembered to bring the great big stereo we had to carry around with us if we wanted to listen to music. Luckily for us, Iron Maiden were huge Hammers fans and we once met Steve Harris when he came to the training ground. Great memories.

And so here we were, two decades later, about to be reunited in our love for West Ham by returning to the club. It was the most fantastic moment – and it also led to future coaching roles for me at West Brom and Watford, when Slav got the top job at those clubs.

I loved coaching because you didn't get all the manager's problems that Slav had to deal with. I quickly established good relationships with all the players, who were as good as gold.

Going back to Chadwell Heath was also a surreal moment for me. Again, in many ways it hadn't changed a single bit. There might have been the odd extra Portakabin that had been stuck in, but otherwise it felt like it was exactly the same. I was well aware that this wasn't the best training facility in the world, but it had its own charm, and I loved it.

The following year we moved to West Ham's new training ground at Rush Green, which was also in Romford. Don't get me wrong, that place was amazing, with superb facilities, and it was probably what the club needed in terms of taking things to the next level, but there was something quite clinical about it, and it was missing the character of Chadwell Heath.

That old place will forever be synonymous with Moore, Hurst and Peters, all of whom trained there. It had the history that was part of its appeal for me. That's why coaching at Chadwell Heath always felt so special to me, because of the heritage of the place.

Unfortunately, poor old Charlie was no longer on the gate, and that wasn't the only difference. For starters, I couldn't believe the sheer number of people who were part of the West Ham set-up. It was mind boggling to someone like me, who had played professional football when there was a manager, his assistant, the physio and the club doctor. And that was more or less the entire backroom team.

Now, the coaching staff alone was enormous and there were analysts for pretty much everything – they even had throw-in analysts. For someone who played in the era I did, it was weird, but I understand that times change. My concern was that sometimes players can get bogged down with being given too much information about what they need to do, instead of just going out and playing.

No manager ever told me what I needed to do when I played, that's not how it was done. But times had changed, and this was how players prepared for games now.

It took a lot of getting used to for me, as did the way the players trained. For starters, I never saw a single fight at training. There was a lot of shouting, but that was it. And I'm not sure if all the players actually enjoyed their training, in the way that we all did. As soon as I came off the pitch at training, I was already looking forward to going back out there the next day. It was all I wanted to do. But maybe that was just me. It could be that I was a bit odd like that.

The dressing room was a different place as well. The players weren't cutting each other's clothes up, or letting down tyres in the car park, but that's fair enough. Strictly speaking, I'm not sure that was entirely necessary in any era. But it was the headphones that were the biggest difference as players were able to shut themselves off in their own worlds, even when they were on the coach, or in the changing room. It was a very different way of doing things, but as it got closer to kick-off, the headphones would come off and the stereo would go on. I may not have liked the music, but that was when it became more familiar, with players psyching each other up, and getting pumped up and ready to play.

One thing I wouldn't let the boys get away with was not acknowledging the fans after the game, whether we'd won, lost or drawn. I was on the pitch reminding them about their duty, because I felt that connection was more important than ever before, at a time when the players were earning big money and driving incredibly expensive cars.

They shouldn't have needed the prompt, but I was there to give it to them anyway, as I loved those fans, so there was no way I was going to allow them to be forgotten.

So much had changed, it was all a bit of a shock to the system. I thoroughly enjoyed being back at West Ham, but I also had to get used to what was a completely different game. Having said all that, I have to say those West Ham players were absolutely magnificent and that last season at

Upton Park was fantastic. It felt like there was a strong connection between the fans and the players, as everyone knew this was the end of an era, and our time at Upton Park was coming to a close.

And it resulted in a great campaign where we finished seventh in the Premier League. Dimitri Payet made a huge impact that season, and he was a really nice lad as well. He worked very hard in training, always staying on the pitch when everyone else had left in order to take a load of free-kicks.

Unfortunately, his time at the club didn't end well as I don't think he went about things the right way and Slav did the right thing by going public about it. No one player is bigger than any club – that's one thing that hadn't changed from the time when I played.

The club captain was Mark Noble, an incredible servant to West Ham who became part of the furniture at the club. It was a huge honour when Mark asked me to play in his testimonial as well.

Slav also gave a young lad called Declan Rice his debut that season, when he was only 18. I still use Declan as an example to kids I coach now, when I'm explaining the importance of not giving the ball away. Declan is the kind of player who does all the simple things right. He'll break up play, make a pass, and make sure his team keeps possession of the ball. And he does all that without doing anything spectacular, making the game look very simple.

Watching every game from the dugout was a strange experience, especially at Upton Park, where I was so used to playing. I wasn't the type of guy who'd scream and shout from the side of the pitch, that just wasn't me. I used to watch each game quietly, carefully observing how we were playing, who was performing well and who was not, and if Slav wanted to talk any of it through, then I'd have a chat with him. But I was as calm then as I was in the dressing room before matches.

My thoughts could often turn to playing, and I couldn't help but think just how painfully slow the football was sometimes. The ball gets passed out at the back, then it goes forward, then it comes back again. It made me think I'd have half a chance if I was still playing, although I'm sure I'd get sent off even more than I used to.

Our second season was very different as it coincided with the move to a new training ground and, of course, the switch to playing in the London Stadium. The changes were really hard for the players. Our first few games had to be played away because the stadium wasn't ready, and when we did finally start playing there, I think it took everyone by surprise.

Suddenly, the fans were much further away from the pitch. We'd gone from that intimidating, compact atmosphere of the Boleyn ground to playing in a vast stadium that you could have put two Upton Parks in. The atmosphere didn't compare to what everyone was used to, though it did improve when we played the likes of Chelsea, Tottenham or Man United.

It was a far cry from Upton Park, where we'd all had the most incredible and emotional end to the previous season, when we faced Man United in our final home game, the last ever to be played at that iconic ground. It was a day that I'll never forget as long as I live.

Not only had fate decreed that I would be back at West Ham for their last season at Upton Park, but also that the final ever fixture there would be against Man United, the team I'd probably enjoyed facing the most at home during my 11 years with the Hammers.

It was too good to be true, a real fairytale ending. We'd all stayed in the team hotel overnight, which was in Canary Wharf. Everyone was understandably pumped up for the game, and raring to get to the stadium, but what should have been a 15-minute drive took us 45 minutes because there were so many people everywhere. Clearly, it wasn't only ticket holders who had come to the farewell party, as many fans had probably decided to come down, soak up the atmosphere, and say farewell.

As we drove through the crowded streets, the scenes were unreal. It was like driving through a carnival, a celebration of West Ham, and the ground that meant so much to everyone. And this was still about an hour and a half before kick-off. Were it not for the fact that I was on the coach with the team and had a job to do, I would have loved to have been out there with the fans. I've seen videos from inside the Boleyn that day, and it looked superb.

When we finally arrived at the stadium, we couldn't actually get the coach to the car park to get us into the ground because the roads were so full. So, we all had to get out of the coach and then walk through the car park and into the ground. I don't think any of us minded at all, as it helped us to feel some of that special atmosphere and get even more pumped up for the game.

We had to hold it back for a bit though as the game was delayed by 45 minutes because Man United's coach had got stuck in the traffic and mayhem outside. It just gave everyone a bit more time to soak it all up.

When I eventually made my way out to the pitchside just before kick-off, the atmosphere inside Upton Park was even better. It was proper hairs-on-the-back-of-your-neck-raising stuff, possibly the loudest I'd ever heard it. I looked around the ground to see the most beautiful sight as the entire stadium had turned claret and blue thanks to the free t-shirts the club had given out.

Just before that, we'd heard the most emotional rendition of 'Bubbles' that almost brought a tear to my eye. When I took my seat in the dugout, all sorts of memories flashed through my mind from my playing career at this most special place. It was so important to me that it ended on a high, and at 2–1 down, it started to look like that might not happen.

Amazingly, the boys turned it around with Winston Reid scoring the winner 10 minutes from the end, and the place went wild. At the final whistle, I remember joining Slav and a couple of the other coaches for a huge group hug.

The club then put on a firework display for the fans, as former players were brought on to the pitch in specially branded 'Final game at the Boleyn' London cabs. They'd asked me to go in one, but I wasn't interested in doing that. That wasn't my style at all. I was happy to be there as a coach on that particular day. That was enough of an honour for me. And as joyous and perfect as the day was, it was also completely heart-breaking.

Leaving the ground for the last time was one of the hardest things to do, because I knew that the next time I came back here, it just wouldn't exist. I know that some of the fans left with all sorts of souvenirs like seats, signs and maybe a few blades of grass. I didn't take anything because I already had something that was incredibly special to me that nobody could ever take away. I had my memories. From smashing in penalties and free kicks, to making those firm but fair (and not so fair) challenges that delighted the fans, I had everything that I needed.

Even though I knew it was coming, I still couldn't believe that was it for Upton Park. No more Nathan's, no more Ken's. All those memories, all those players, and all those magnificent fans. It still brings a lump to my throat just thinking about it, and that's why I continue to visit the site of the ground as often as I can, because I just love being there. Even when it's not there, I know that it was. And I know that it was real because I lived and breathed it, just like the fans did.

That magical final day at the Boleyn was only topped by one other memory, which happened a month or two earlier. And that was when I played for West Ham at Upton Park again for one last time.

•

I pull on the blue West Ham shirt, and I can hardly believe what I'm doing. It's been 16 years since I last played at this ground, and here I am right now, in the changing room, ready to go on to that hallowed turf again.

I sit down on the bench and look around. I've got a huge smile on my face, as I see Steve Lomas, Anton and Rio Ferdinand, David James, Craig Bellamy, Carlton Cole, Yossi Benayoun, all sitting around me.

This is completely unreal. I feel like I'm in proper pinch-yourself territory as I pull on my boots and start lacing them up. The boots that are going to tread on the grass on that pitch again. What a feeling this is.

As always, I haven't warmed up, but I've also not had my Coke and Mars in the bath either. Those days are gone.

I get up off the bench with my boots on and start clattering around the changing room floor. I can still feel my knee.

I've never not felt it. I'm not going to last 90 minutes today. I'm not even going to make 45.

When Mark Noble asked me to play in his testimonial, I was touched. It meant the world to me to have one more chance to play at the Boleyn. But I had to tell him that I struggle to walk, never mind play football, so 20 minutes would be the most I'd be able to manage.

But I'm good with that. I pace around the changing room and I know that just to have the opportunity to do this is so special. It doesn't matter that I'm in my late forties. I still just want to play football, and to play at this ground in front of these fans all these years later is a dream come true.

The buzzer goes. It's just like old times. Rio leads us out as he's the skipper today and I follow on behind. There's lots of banter between us. I'm beaming from ear to ear, loving every second of this.

We go past all the memories on the walls of the tunnel again, like I do before every home game. But I'm the coach in those games, so I don't do this bit with the players. But today, right now, I am, and it's a special feeling.

All those memories. Bobby Moore, Billy Bonds, Trevor Brooking, through to the more modern-day stories of playoff wins. And now this moment that I'm living through right now, which will turn into another of those memories soon enough.

Up the stairs I go, and now I'm out on the pitchside, and there are bubbles everywhere, and the fans are in full voice.

Because this is a testimonial, we line up and form a guard of honour for Mark Noble to walk through. He's delayed his arrival so that he can have the moment he deserves, the moment I had myself about 16 years ago.

I look up and see that the stadium is packed. It doesn't look like there's a single empty seat and I love those fans just a bit more.

Alongside me are the 'all stars' who I'm playing alongside today, and opposite me are the players I coach every day, who'll be playing against us. Everyone's smiling and looking towards the tunnel, waiting for Mark to emerge.

Here he comes now. He walks out, holding hands with his children who accompany him on to the pitch and through the space we have formed for him. We all clap, and the whole stadium rises as one to join in with the appreciation of a loyal club servant.

I was that man once. In many ways, I still am. Back for another spell to serve the fans I love so much.

Mark heads into the centre circle to wave to all the fans, and we all continue clapping. He's getting the ovation he fully deserves.

Now, we all move towards our own halves of the pitch. As I walk across to take up my usual position on the left, I feel my boots walking on this beautiful grass again. It's like a miracle.

Again, I take in the surroundings. I'm looking at all the fans, but from the perspective of being back on the pitch again, here in my left-back berth that I know so well, but where I haven't stood for so long.

I'm getting loads of cheers and shouts from the fans closest to me. I give them a wave and a smile. The atmosphere is so warm and friendly. I feel like I'm with family when I'm out here.

In the centre circle, the ref looks around the pitch and seems ready to get us started. He blows his whistle and we're off. I'm playing at Upton Park again, just weeks before it won't even exist anymore. Here I am. One last chance.

To be honest, it's not that easy for me to get up and down the pitch in my own half, never mind getting further forward in the opposition half. My knee will only allow me to do so much.

But I don't care about that knee now. I just want to enjoy this and worry about any pain later.

I look along the defensive line and see Rio and Anton Ferdinand in the middle, and Mark Ward over on the right. What a sight that is.

Michail Antonio is approaching with the ball and I just can't resist. I can't steam straight through him, I'm not sure I'm capable of that. Plus, I don't want to injure one of my own players. But I can just about get to that ball first, and clatter into him. So I do that, and he tumbles over.

Everyone loves it. I don't know if Michail does, but it doesn't matter too much. He'll be ok. Meanwhile the ball that I won has gone forward, and suddenly Craig Bellamy's got it, and strokes an absolute beauty into the corner of the net. I'll have the assist on that one, thank you very much.

Everyone's laughing and smiling. This is football purely for the joy of the game. And it really is a beautiful game.

Now, Mark Noble is dribbling towards our penalty area. I see Rio and Anton letting him through, so I do the same. I stop running, hoping that Mark can enjoy a special moment.

He waltzes all the way through with only David James to beat, but Jamo decides to make a reflex save and stop him from scoring. Fair enough, he wants to enjoy his day too, and not just stand there and let goal after goal in.

I get the feeling that Mark may get one or two more chances as the game goes on.

The game is being played at a gentle pace. Nobody is breaking a serious sweat which is good news for me, seeing as I'm finding it fairly hard going to move with much pace.

I'm not seeing a great deal of the ball but that's ok. I'm just loving playing in front of the fans again.

I look to the touchline where the dugout is, and there are a few substitutes who look ready to enter the fray. Like everything good in life, it feels as if it's gone by so quickly.

Like my 11 years playing here. Like the 16 years since I last played here. It's all happened in the blink of an eye.

I walk over towards them and start clapping the fans. I can see Christian Dailly, Trevor Sinclair, Paolo Di Canio and Danny Gabbidon all waiting to come on.

My number is up. And so are Wardy's, Scott Parker's and Stewart Downing's, and they all leave the pitch to a warm reception from the fans.

I continue clapping the fans as I approach the white line that separates the players from everyone else.

It's a line I used to be honoured to cross on behalf of West Ham every week.

And as I walk back across that white line for the last time, I'm so happy I've had the privilege to have played here in front of all these fans again, even if it's only been for 20 minutes.

My career was cut short at 29. It was the cruellest of blows. But that doesn't mean I didn't love every second of the time I had. As I sit down on the bench, I'm a very happy Hammer.

Acknowledgements

Family comes first, so I'll start by thanking my mum and dad for bringing me into this world. My dad was a semi-pro footballer in Bristol so that's where I get my footballing genes from, while I'd also like to thank my mum for screaming her head off on the touchline every Saturday and Sunday when I was a kid, and then at Upton Park when I was a pro.

A huge thank you to my daughters Kattie and Jessica, who kept me on my toes, and Eliyanah, my two-year-old who still does. I can't imagine life without them, and my grandson Teddy.

And my partner Lisa who always supports me and puts up with all my mood swings – believe me I have many, and I know that I am lucky to have her.

I'd also like to thank my brother Grantley for our competitiveness – we used to kick the shit out of each other and that probably helped me in my career at one or two points.

Also, to my nan and grandads for always being there for me and loving me unconditionally.

On the football front, thanks to Ron Veal, the scout who spotted me playing for my school side at the age of 11 and eventually took me to Aston Villa and Birmingham. Also to his wife Mabel, who was a beautiful person and always made us feel welcome.

Ron Saunders gave me my first opportunity at Birmingham. He was a great figure in my life as a schoolboy and a young pro. At the same time as that, I have to thank Janet and Brian Rodgers who were my surrogate mum and dad in Birmingham as I left home at 14 and lived in digs. They were special, special people.

John Bond managed me at Birmingham and he always urged his teams to play football. To me, he was a special manager.

John Lyall brought me to West Ham so I will forever be indebted to him. He was a very special person and in my opinion was way ahead of his footballing time. Thanks to him, I had 11 magnificent years at West Ham, with quite a lot of ups and downs, but overall it was an unbelievable time for me. As long as you played for the Hammers, there was no better place to play football than Upton Park.

Many West Ham fans won't like me for this, but I have to thank Lou Macari, who did wonders for my career by making me captain, penalty taker, free-kick taker and made me go up for corners.

I may have had many rows with Billy Bonds, but the greatest compliment I can pay him is, if I had to pick one player to go to war alongside, it would definitely be Billy.

I loved Graeme Souness as a manager and a person. Even though I initially didn't want to go to Liverpool, I thank him for taking me there and giving me the opportunity to play at a magnificent stadium and for one of the biggest clubs in the world.

Harry Redknapp was the greatest there was in terms of man management. He made you feel like you were the best player in your position, and got the best out of many players.

I've shared rooms with many great players that have become friends, but I want to take the opportunity to mention one in particular, Slaven Bilic. He's one of the most genuine and humble men in football. I want to thank him for believing in me as a coach and giving me many opportunities in football, at West Ham, West Brom and Watford, something not many people have done. Funnily enough, he used to make my coffee back in the day and I ended up making his.

I'd like to thank all the players who gave up their time to tell stories about me, including Martin Allen, Tony Gale, Frank McAvennie and Kenny Brown.

And a huge thank you to the publisher Jonathan Taylor for believing in my book and wanting to tell my stories, to Gershon my ghost writer, with whom I had some laughs along the way. And finally, thanks to Jason Finegan, my agent, for setting up the opportunity to write this book in the first place.

Last, but by no means least, thank you to all the West Ham fans for the unwavering support during and after my career. You're all very special people.